Acquisition.cc

$100M Offers Summary and Workbook

How To Make Offers So Good People Feel Stupid Saying No

ALEX HORMOZI

Acquisition.com, LLC
7710 N FM 620
Building 13C, Suite 100
Austin, TX 78726

Acquisition.com

$100M Offers Summary and Workbook

How To Make Offers So Good People Feel Stupid Saying No

By

ALEX HORMOZI

WHY I MADE THIS WORKBOOK & SUMMARY

Owning businesses with hundreds of millions (not a typo) in yearly revenue taught me many things. But, it taught me one important thing in particular. Success doesn't come to those who talk about business, it comes to those who *do* business. And you *do* business by using business skills to do actual business stuff.

In my experience, most people already understand the nuts and bolts of business:

- Make or get something to sell.

- Let people know you have a thing to sell.

- Offer that thing to people interested in buying it.

- Make more money than it costs to sell and deliver the thing.

- Use leftover money to pay yourself and grow the business.

- Repeat.

They just get stuck on the *how* of business. *HOW* can you do all that stuff? *Skills*.

I became successful at business…

- Not because I have secrets.

- Not because I invented something revolutionary.

- Not because I'm the only one who makes more money than I spend.

- But because I invested everything I could into building the skills of business.

I also know investing into business skills prevents you from investing into other stuff. But I respect this choice. And I respect you for doing it because *you make a good investment.* When it pays off, everything you put in can come back to you 5x, 10x, 100x, 1000x or more. Then, you can put resources into whatever you want (including more business stuff!) at an *insane* rate.

I made the *$100M* books, workbooks, and courses because *you chose that path*. I know business skills get difficult to master. I know they take lots of reps to master. I also know you *can* master them. This workbook gives you another piece to that puzzle.

I know the principles in these books helped me. But, for the sake of the mission, I quietly collected proof that they worked for others, too. It took some time, but the feedback says it all. Since I began the mission to make real business education accessible to everyone it has affected millions. I see the teenager door-knocking. The dad at his carwash. The gardener in her stall at the farmer's market. They've all taken me aside to tell me how the principles worked for them.

The sheer number of people who stop me on the street every day to tell me "I learned a new skill"… "I can feed my family"… "I tripled my income"… "I actually have a reason to get up in the morning"… All shake me to my core. Every time.

I made the *$100M* books, workbooks, and free courses for *you*. The one who wants to win at the game of business. These principles apply to you if you've already established yourself, as I have. They also apply if you've lost everything and hit rock bottom, as I have (twice).

This workbook summarizes all the important stuff in the main book, strengthens your understanding of it, and puts your new-found knowledge to the test. You will find it simple *and* effective… so long as you do it.

I credit these principles - and the skills that came from them - for the majority of my success.

And, as the years go on, they've proven to work for others.

Now, they can work for you.

WHAT THIS IS NOT

Now you know why I made this workbook and summary. But, I also want you to keep your eye on the prize. So, I will close the loop by telling you what this workbook is *not*.

This Workbook Does NOT Try To Sound Fancy

If you want fancy armchair analysis from eggheads. Go somewhere else.

If you want fancy math and fancy words. Go somewhere else.

If you want fancy fluff that'll distract you from making money. Go somewhere else.

I see book critics slam simple language and simple approaches. They also almost never have big successful businesses. So while they get jollies from finding tiny typos you can get jollies from building big bank accounts. I know complicated stuff and fancy jargon entertains people. But, simple principles stated in plain English will *make you rich*. And I care about making you rich.

Some people act snobbish about this stuff. Let them. More for us.

This Workbook Does NOT "Innovate"

These principles aren't mine - they came from business itself.

You may have heard, read, or seen many of the things I say in other places. *Good.* The more places you see solid business principles, the better. I only give you my flavor, my experiences, and the ever-growing successes of people who adopted them as I have.

This workbook doesn't break any ground. I don't want it to. I present big ideas in simple ways and make sure you know them well enough to use them. Some suggest strange and complicated business stuff that really depends on luck - all in the name of "innovation." I suggest simple and proven stuff that depends on *hard work*. Then, *when* you find something that makes you money, you double down and *work even harder*.

Yes, luck *does* play a role in business. Your business will have seasons for that reason. But, hard work pays *whether you've got luck on your side or not*. Then, *when* your luck comes, your hard work compounds into something incredible. It all comes together.

Successful business owners think in decades, not days. Some seasons look great and others not so much. But, when you see all the seasons put next to each other, results speak for themselves.

This Workbook Is NOT Written By A Man Who Hasn't Done Everything In It

Rarely do I talk about my formal education. Yes, I studied business at Vanderbilt. No, I don't think it made a difference one way or the other. I met thousands of people with fancy business degrees who have gone nowhere with them. The degree itself means nothing.

I don't talk about business because I know stuff *about* business.

I talk about business because I *do* it.

I have done business and won.

I have done business and lost it all.

I have done business and won again.

All the stuff in the books, courses, and workbooks - I've lived it.

This Workbook Is NOT The Main Book

When I first started these workbooks I had an issue. Most of the other workbooks out there sucked. They copied some stuff from one book, pasted it into another, asked a stupid open-ended question, then added dozens of blank pages to "reflect." *Sucky fluff to the max.*

If I published sucky fluff… I could never live with myself. It does wrong by you and everyone else who cares about this mission. The *$100M* Series have done a fantastic job on their own. Putting out the same stuff again would look lame, cannibalize my own content *and* insult you. Gross.

The workbook, although the ultimate companion to the *$100M* Series, had to stand on its own.

The workbook brings together important concepts - but it is not the main book.

The workbook strengthens your understanding of those concepts - but it is not the main book.

The workbook challenges you to apply those concepts - but it is not the main book.

The workbook does raise your money making potential - but it is not the main book.

The workbook *can* stand on its own but…

If you use the workbook to replace the main book *you might make a mistake.*

The main book makes the workbook more valuable.

The workbook makes the main book more valuable.

So to get the biggest benefits to your business - *use both.*

This Workbook Is NOT For People Who Think Making Lots Of Money Is Bad

So many good people have the wrong beliefs about money.

They think making lots of money, or wanting to, makes them bad people. They think others will see them as bad if they try. And, for that reason, many good people keep themselves poor… on purpose!

Let me tell you something.

When the good guys keep themselves poor on purpose, the bad guys win.

End of story.

Getting good at business also means getting the right beliefs about money. Like it or not, a business has one primary function - to make it. As a business owner, if you put making money anywhere other than the top of your list, your business will fail. The good guys lose. Don't let the good guys lose.

Business has tons of virtuous elements:

Mastering skills, building self-control, distributing useful stuff, and making a difference in people's lives. If you take money-making out of the equation, like many naive business owners do- *it all falls apart.*

Good businesses make lots of money.

If you want to build a good business, then get comfortable making lots of money.

Let's make lots of money.

HOW TO USE THIS WORKBOOK & SUMMARY

You can use this workbook and summary…

- On its own

- Before reading the main book

- After reading the main book

- While reading the main book.

So really you can use the workbook whenever you want.

The workbook goes over material in the same order as the main book. This makes it easier to go through both books at once - but the similarities end there.

First, I go over an important business thing. I introduce this important business thing as a problem to solve a "key concept" and the like. You'll know it when you see it. Second, I give an example of that important stuff in action and maybe a few other notes about it. After that, you do an exercise (or several) about the key concept to help it stick. Then, where it makes sense, you see how it makes a difference in your business. This process repeats for each important business thing I stuffed in here.

But only one thing really matters, that you *use the stuff in real life.*

OUTLINE OF THIS WORKBOOK + SUMMARY

I hate seeing people led astray. I saw 30+ people making <u>bad workbooks</u> out of an objectively great book (based on the 20,000+ 5-star Amazon reviews). And since some people only read workbooks and summaries, they would judge me off the poor bastardized versions of my book. That felt bad. So, I decided to make a workbook + summary version of my original book $100M Offers myself. At least this way, you learn the right stuff rather than whatever some person who never owned a business *tells you* is important. You can hear it from me.

I simplified the original text into a problem solution framework for you.

Intro:

Problem A: Why can Alex give advice? →Solution A: Credibility & Relatability

Problem B: Business Owners are Broke→Solution B: They need a Grand Slam Offer

How to make a Grand Slam Offer:

Problem #1: You Sell a Commodity→Solution #1: Differentiate

Problem #2: You Have Bad Customers→Solution #2: Find a Starving Crowd

Problem #3: You Price Too Low To Make Money→ Solution #3: Premium Pricing

Problem #4: Your Thing Isn't Valuable→ Solution #4: Make It Valuable

Problem #5: You're Solving The Wrong Way→ Solution #5: Solve The Right Way

Problem #6: You're Solving The Wrong Problems→ Solve The Right Problems

Offer Enhancers

The components

Problem #7: People Still Aren't Buying→ Solution #7: Add Scarcity

Problem #8: People Still Aren't Buying→ Solution #8: Add Urgency

Problem #9: People Still Aren't Buying→ Solution #9: Add Bonuses

Problem #10: People Still Aren't Buying→ Solution #10: Add Guarantees

Problem #11: The Wrong People Are Buying→ Solution #11: Change The Name

Problem #12: Nothing's Happening→ Solution #12: Make it Happen

Execute

By the end of this workbook, I will solve all 12 problems with your current offer. Together we will transform it into a grand slam offer. This tends to result in buckets of money descending upon you with increased frequency and intensity.

Let's dive in.

Table of Contents

INTRO 1

Problem A: Why can Alex give advice? → Solution A: Credibility & Relatability 3

Problem B: Business Owners are Broke → Solution B: They need a Grand Slam Offer .. 5

HOW TO MAKE A GRAND SLAM OFFER 7

Problem #1: You Sell a Commodity → Solution #1: Differentiate 7

Problem #2: You Have Bad Customers → Solution #2: Find a Starving Crowd 15

Problem #3: You Price Too Low To Make Money → Solution #3: Premium Pricing 23

Problem #4: Your Thing Isn't Valuable → Solution #4: Make It Valuable 29

Problem #5: You're Solving The Wrong Way → Solution #5: Solve The Right Way 43

Problem #6: You're Solving The Wrong Problems→ Solution #6: Solve the Right Problems . 47

ENHANCING YOUR GRAND SLAM OFFER 63

Problem #7: People Still Aren't Buying → Solution #7: Add Scarcity 65

Problem #8: People Still Aren't Buying → Solution #8: Add Urgency 69

Problem #9: People Still Aren't Buying → Solution #9: Add Bonuses 73

Problem #10: People Still Aren't Buying → Solution #10: Add Guarantees 79

Problem #11: The Wrong People Are Buying → Solution #11: Change The Name 91

Problem #12: Nothing's Happening → Solution #12: Make It Happen 99

FREE GOODIES 103

INTRO

"Outsized returns often come from betting against conventional wisdom, and conventional wisdom is usually right. Given a 10 percent chance of a 100 times payoff, you should take that bet every time. But you're still going to be wrong nine times out of ten . . . We all know that if you swing for the fences, you're going to strike out a lot, but you're also going to hit some home runs. The difference between baseball and business, however, is that baseball has a truncated outcome distribution. When you swing, no matter how well you connect with the ball, the most runs you can get is four. In business, every once in a while, when you step up to the plate, you can score 1,000 runs. This long-tailed distribution of returns is why it's important to be bold. Big winners pay for so many experiments."

— **Jeff Bezos**

As entrepreneurs, we make bets everyday. We are gamblers – gambling our hard-earned money on labor, inventory, rent, marketing, etc., all with the hopes of a higher payout. Oftentimes, we lose. But, sometimes, we win and win BIG. However, there is a difference between gambling in business and gambling in a casino. In a casino, the odds are stacked against you. With skill, you can improve them, but never beat them. In contrast, in business, you can improve your skills to shift the odds in your favor. Simply stated, with enough skill, you can become the house.

After beginning a series of books on acquisition, it became apparent that I could not talk about any other topic without first addressing *the offer*: the starting point of any conversation to initiate a transaction with a customer. What you are literally *providing* them in exchange for their money. That's where it all begins.

This book is about how to make profitable offers. Specifically, how to *reliably* turn advertising dollars into (enormous) profits using a combination of pricing, value, guarantees, and naming strategies. I call the proper combination of these components: a *Grand Slam Offer*.

I chose this term partially in homage to the above quote from Amazon founder Jeff Bezos and because, like a grand slam in baseball, a Grand Slam Offer is both very good and very rare. Additionally, to extend the baseball metaphor, it takes no more effort to make a Grand Slam Offer than to strike out. The difference is dictated by the skill of the marketer and how well he connects his offer with his audience's desires. In business you can have so-so offers: the "singles" and "doubles' that keep the game going, pay the bills, and keep the lights on. But, unlike baseball, where a grand slam scores a maximum of four runs, a Grand Slam Offer in the business world, can score you a thousand-fold payoff and result in a world where you never need to work again. It would be like connecting with the ball so well during one single at bat that you automatically win every World Series for the next hundred years.

It takes years of practice to make something as complicated as hitting a major league fastball into the bleachers look effortless. Your stance, vision, prediction, ball speed, bat speed, and hip placement all must be perfect. In marketing and customer acquisition (the process of getting new clients), there are just as many variables that must all align to truly "knock it out of the park." But with enough practice and enough skill, you can turn the wild world of acquisition, which *will* throw curveballs at you everyday, into a home run derby, knocking offer after offer out of the stadium. To everyone else, your success will look unbelievable. But to you, it will feel like "just another day at work." The greatest hitters of all time also have many strike outs, just as there are many failed offers in the track record of great marketers. We learn skills through failure and practice. We do this knowing that nine out of ten times we will be wrong. We still act boldly, hoping for that offer we connect with so well that it results in our big payoff.

The good news is that in business, you only need to hit *one* Grand Slam Offer to retire forever. I have done this four or five times in my life. As for my track record, I have a 36:1 lifetime return on my advertising dollars over my business career. Consider this my lifetime "batting average," if you will. That means for every $1 I spend on advertising I get $36 back, a 3600% return. That is my average over eight years. And I continue to improve.

This book is my attempt to share that skill with you, with a specific focus on building Grand Slam Offers, so you can experience the same levels of success. It's also the first in a series of books meant to get entrepreneurs to financial freedom, in plain words, "eff you" money. Subsequent books in this series will look more deeply at getting more customers, converting more prospects into clients, making those clients worth more, and other lessons I wish I had learned earlier scaling my businesses.

Problem A: Why can Alex give advice?
→ Solution A: Credibility & Relatability

Relatability

I started my entrepreneurial career sleeping on the floor of a gym because I didn't have enough money for two rents. I eventually grew that to 6 locations. Then I lost all my money the first time with a bad partnership (story in $100M Offers). Then I started over again doing a turnkey gym turnaround business. 32 turnarounds in two years. Things looked good until I lost all my money a second time due to a processing mishap (story in $100M Offers). Yes, I've lost all my money *twice*. So I know what it's like to have nothing with your back against the wall. I failed/closed nine businesses in my career before making my first really big one.

Credibility

My first really big one - Gym Launch - was a gym licensing company. We grew it to over 5000+ locations. I sold it (and its sister company Prestige Labs) for $46.2M at age 31. I had taken out ~$40,000,000 in owner earnings before selling it. I crossed $100M in net worth by age 32. I'm now an investor with a portfolio of companies that do $200,000,000 per year.

What kept me alive in the early days - and has kept my companies growing since then - has been my ability to make grand slam offers (the subject of this workbook).

Intention

My investment portfolio is my day job. Making content for entrepreneurs is my side hustle. I make the content to attract business owners so that I can invest in their companies and help them grow. I usually only do deals with companies over ~$3,000,000 in annual profit. For everyone else, I just hope your life gets better from these lessons that took me far too much pain to learn.

If you have a business, go to acquisition.com to see if we can help you grow.

Problem B: Business Owners are Broke
→ Solution B: They need a Grand Slam Offer

How I learned about making grand slam offers

When I was 23 years old, I paid for a weekend workshop from a business guru. I had never run a business before, nor had I marketed. I didn't know how to make money. The guru, seeing how lost I felt, called me over during the break. He said "do you want to know the secret to sales…?" I nodded and leaned in "…make people an offer so good they'd feel stupid saying no."

This is where I learned that if I just made people incredible offers, I could win. I didn't have to be an amazing marketer. I didn't have to be an amazing salesperson. I could just make incredible offers - which I have coined "grand slam offers" - and make money.

> MAKE PEOPLE AN OFFER SO GOOD THEY WOULD FEEL STUPID SAYING NO.

What's An Offer Anyways?

The *only* way to conduct business is through a value exchange, a trade of dollars for value. The offer is what initiates this trade. In a nutshell, the offer is the goods and services you agree to give or provide, how you accept payment, and the terms of the agreement. It is what *begins* the process of getting customers and making money. It is the first thing any new customer will interact with in your business. Since the offer is what attracts new customers, it is the lifeblood of your business.

The Two Main Problems Most Entrepreneurs Face and How This Book Solves Them

Although you *can* make the list of problems you face a mile long, which is a great way to stress yourself out, all these problems typically stem from two big kahunas:

1) Not enough clients

2) Not enough cash (excess profit at the end of the month)

Making a Grand Slam Offer solves both. You get more leads, more sales, at higher prices, with even higher profits. In short, if everyone wants your super valuable thing, then you will get lots of people to shell over their cash to get it. This beats haggling over pennies with very few people who don't want what you have. Better, right? Right.

This concludes the intro. Now we go into the problems and solutions most businesses have with their offers.

HOW TO MAKE A GRAND SLAM OFFER

Problem #1: You Sell a Commodity → Solution #1: Differentiate

"Think different."
— Steve Jobs

Value-Driven vs. Price-Driven Purchases

Having a Grand Slam Offer helps with all *three* of the requirements for growth: getting more customers, getting them to pay more, and getting them to do so more times.

How? It allows you to differentiate yourself from the marketplace. In other words, it allows you to sell your product based on VALUE not on PRICE.

Commoditized = Price Driven Purchases (race to the bottom)

Differentiated = Value Driven Purchases (sell in a category of one with no comparison. Yes, market matters, which I'll explain in the next chapter)

A commodity, as I define it, is *a product available from many places*. For that reason, it's prone to purchases based on "price" instead of "value." If all products are "equal," then the cheapest one is the most valuable by default. In other words, if a prospect compares your product to another and thinks "these are pretty much the same, I'll buy the cheaper one," then they commoditized you. How embarrassing! But really . . . it's one of the worst experiences a value-driven entrepreneur can have.

This is a massive problem for the entrepreneur because commodities are valued at the point of market efficiency. This means that the marketplace drives the price down through competition until the margins are *just* enough to keep the lights on: "just enough" to become a slave to their business. The business makes "just enough" to justify the owner waiting anxiously for things to "turn around," and by the time that lie is realized . . . they are in too deep to pivot (at least, until now).

A Grand Slam Offer solves this problem.

EXERCISE #1: Price vs Value Driven Purchases

Circle the letter P or V to indicate which of the following was a price driven purchase (P) or value driven purchase (V):

- Looking at different supplement brands on Amazon (P / V)
- Seeing an email with an offer you hadn't thought of but now want (P / V)
- Door to door salesman offers to sell you solar (P / V)
- At shopping mart looking at brands of milk (P / V)
- Calling up different ad agencies to get their prices (P / V)
- Buying gas at the gas station (P / V)
- Buying a one-of-a-kind marriage retreat after seeing an ad (P / V)

What Does A Grand Slam Offer Change?

Let's start by defining a Grand Slam Offer.

It's an offer you present to the marketplace that cannot be compared to any other product or service available. This forces a value *rather than* a price based buying decision.

It combines an attractive promotion, an unmatchable value proposition, a premium price, and an unbeatable guarantee with a money model (payment terms) that allows you to *get paid* to get new customers . . . forever removing the cash constraint on business growth.

In other words, it allows you to sell in a "category of one," or, to apply another great phrase, to "sell in a vacuum." The resulting purchasing decision for the prospect is now between your product *and nothing*. So you can sell at whatever price you get the prospect to perceive, not in comparison to anything else. As a result, it gets you more customers, at higher ticket prices, for less money. If you like fancy marketing terms, it breaks down like this:

1) <u>Increased Response Rates (think clicks)</u>

2) <u>Increased Conversion (think sales)</u>

3) <u>Premium Prices (think charging a lot of money)</u>.

Having a Grand Slam Offer increases your response rates to advertisements (aka more people will click or take an action on an advertisement they see containing a Grand Slam Offer).

If you pay the same amount for eyeballs but 1) more people respond, 2) more of those responses buy, and 3) they buy for higher prices, your business *grows*.

<u>Here's the key takeaway from all this</u>: a business does the *same* work in both cases (with a commoditized or a Grand Slam Offer). The fulfillment is the same. But if one business uses a Grand Slam Offer and another uses a "commodity" offer, the Grand Slam Offer makes that business appear as if it has a totally different product — and that means a value-driven, versus price-driven, purchase.

If you have a "commodity" offer, you will compete on price (having a price-driven purchase versus a value-driven purchase). Your Grand Slam Offer, however, forces a prospect to stop and *think differently* to assess the value of your differentiated product. Doing this establishes you as your own category, which means it's too difficult to compare prices, which means *you* re-calibrate the prospect's value-meter.

EXERCISE #2: What does a new offer affect?

Check the box for the business functions affected by a new offer:

- ☐ Price
- ☐ Accounting
- ☐ Advertising
- ☐ Sales
- ☐ Human Resources

Real Life Case Study: Grand Slam Offer Before & After (Skip if you're pressed for time)

Three sentence backstory . . . we own a software company that advertising agencies use to work leads for their customers. Using our software, agencies transform their offer from a commoditized offer of lead generation services to a Grand Slam Offer of "pay for performance." Let me show you the multiplicative effect it has on the revenue of the business.

While rounded for illustration's sake, these values are based on the real numbers a lead generation agency selling services to brick and mortar businesses experience

Old Commoditized Way (Price-Driven) — Race to the bottom

Commoditized Offer: $1,000 down, then $1,000/mo retainer for agency services

Metric	Commodity	Grand Slam	Explanation
Advertising Spend	$10,000		Dollars Spent on advertising
Impressions Reached	300,000		Eyeballs reached from advertising
Response Rate	0.00013		Percentage of people who book call (CTR x Optin %)
Appts Booked	40		# of Appointments Booked as a result
Show Rate	75%		Percentage of people who book call
Appts Showed	30		# of people who show up for their appt
Closing %	16%		% of people who purchase
Appts Closed	5		# of people who purchase
Price	$1,000		The amount that people put down to begin service
Total	$5,000		Total amount of up front cash collected
ROAS	.5 : 1		Return on Advertising Spend (ROAS)

Breakdown: At .5 to 1 return on advertising spend, you lose money getting customers. But in 30 days, those 5 customers will pay another $1,000 each, bringing you to $10,000 in total and break even. The next month, the $5,000 that comes in would be your first profitable month, and each month thereafter would be profitable (assuming they all stay).

This is an example of a commoditized service — normal agency work. There's a million of them, and they all look the same. Commoditized businesses and offers have a harder time getting responses from ads because all their marketing looks the same as everyone else's.

> **Note:** It all looks the same because they are all making the same offer.
> *You pay us to work.*
> *We do work.*
> *Maybe you get results from that work. Maybe you don't.*

It's reasonable, but it's easily duplicated (and subject to commoditization). *This commoditization creates a price-driven purchase . . .*

You are forced to be priced "competitively" to get clients *and* to stay that way to keep them. If the client sees a cheaper version of the "same thing," then the value discrepancy will cause them to swap providers. This is a dilemma . . . lose this client, the rest of your clients, and potential clients, or stay "competitive." Your margins become so thin they *vanish*.

Furthermore, it's hard to get prospects to say yes (and *keep* them saying yes) unless you're hypervigilant about clients commoditizing your business by staying "competitive." And that's the problem with the old commoditized way. They're able to compare. Unless you switch to a Grand Slam Offer, your prices will keep getting beaten down. The business eventually dies, or the entrepreneur throws in the towel. No bueno.

We want to make an offer that's so different that you can skip the awkward explanation of why your product is different from everyone else's (which, if they have to ask, then they are probably too ignorant to understand the explanation) and instead just have the offer do that work for you. That's the Grand Slam Offer way.

Let's dive in to see the contrast in sales numbers.

New Grand Slam Offer Way (Differentiated, Incomparable) (Value-Driven)

Grand Slam Offer: Pay one time. (No recurring fee. No retainer.) Just cover ad spend. I'll generate leads and work your leads for you. And only pay me if people show up. And I'll guarantee you get 20 people in your first month, or you get your next month free. I'll also provide all the best practices from other businesses like yours.

- Daily sales coaching for your staff

- Tested scripts

- Tested price points and offers to swipe and deploy

- Sales recordings

. . . and everything else you need to sell and fulfill your customers. I'll give you the entire play book for (insert industry), absolutely free just for becoming a client.

In a nutshell, I'm feeding people into your business, showing you, exactly, how to sell them so that you can get the highest prices, which means that you make the most money possible . . . sound fair enough?

It's clear these are drastically different offers . . . but so what? Where's the *money*!? Let's compare both in the below chart.

Metric	Commodity	Grand Slam	Difference
Advertising Spend	$10,000	$10,000	Unchanged
Impressions Reached	300,000	300,000	Unchanged
Response Rate	0.00013	0.00033	2.5x Response (more appealing, so more respond)
Appts Booked	40	100	Result
Show Rate	75%	75%	Unchanged
Appts Showed	30	75	Result
Closing %	16%	37%	2.3x Closing (more value, so more buy)
Appts Closed	5	28	Result
Price	$1,000	$3,997	4x Price (one time fee vs recurring)
Total	$5,000	$112,000	22.4x Cash Up Front Collected
ROAS	.5 : 1	11.2 : 1	Get paid to get customers.

Breakdown: You spend the same amount of money for the same eyeballs. Then, you get 2.5x more people to respond to your advertisement because it's a more compelling offer. From there, you close 2.5x as many people because the offer is so much more compelling. From there, you are able to charge a 4x higher price up front. The end result is 2.5 x 2.5 x 4 = 22.4x more cash collected up front. Yes, you spent $10,000 to make $112,000. You just *made money* getting new customers.

Comparison: Remember the old way, the way you lost half the ad spend up front? With the new way, you are making *more* money *and* getting *more* customers. This means that your cost to acquire a customer is so cheap (relative to how much you make) that your limiting factor becomes your ability to do the work you already love doing. Cash flow and acquiring customers is no longer your bottleneck because it's 22.4x more profitable than the old model. Yup. You read that right. This is the part in the action movie where you walk away from an explosion in slow motion.

This is the exact Grand Slam Offer we used with our software business that serves agencies. The numbers can become wild . . . fast. I know 22.4x better sounds unreasonable, but that's the point. If you play the same game everyone else does, you'll get the same results everyone else does (mediocre).

When you get this right, the results are, well . . . unbelievable.

Summary Points

- The problem with commoditization and being the same as others

- Price-based buying decisions vs Value-based buying decisions

- The value of a grand slam offer is that you aren't compared to anything else available in the marketplace

- Real world impact of making a grand slam offer

FREE GIFT #1 BONUS TUTORIAL: "START HERE"

If you want a deeper dive, go to **Acquisition.com/ training/offers** and watch the first video in the free course (starring yours truly) about how I differentiate offers in businesses I consult with and get them to charge premium prices. I also created some Free SOPs/Cheat Codes for you to use so you can implement faster. You can also scan the QR Code if you don't like typing. It's absolutely free. Enjoy.

Problem #2: You Have Bad Customers
→ Solution #2: Find a Starving Crowd

A grand slam offer presented to the wrong audience will fall on deaf ears. On the other hand, if you get the market right, you can get everything else wrong and still make money. This chapter focuses on picking the right market.

Half-Page Story

A marketing professor asked his students, "If you were going to open a hotdog stand, and you could only have *one* advantage over your competitors . . . which would it be . . . ?"

"Location! ....Quality! .... Low prices! ....Best taste!"

The students kept going until eventually they had run out of answers. They looked at each other waiting for the professor to speak. The room finally fell quiet.

The professor smiled and replied, *"A starving crowd."*

You could have the worst hot dogs, terrible prices, and be in a terrible location, but if you're the only hot dog stand in town and the local college football game breaks out, you're going to sell out. That's the value of a starving crowd.

At the end of the day, if there is a ton of demand for a solution, you can be mediocre at business, have a terrible offer, and have no ability to persuade people, and you can *still* make money.

An example of this was the toilet paper shortage at the beginning of Covid-19. There was no offer. The pricing was atrocious. And there was no compelling sales pitch. But because the crowd was so big and so starving, rolls of toilet paper were going for $100 or more. That's the value of a starving crowd.

Case Study: Selling Newspapers

Bad Customer Example: One of my friends, Lloyd, owned a software company that converted print advertising products for newspapers into digital ads. He was modernizing an ancient business. He struggled mightily to grow it despite being a great entrepreneur. Main reason: the newspaper industry was shrinking 25 percent per year! No matter how good you are, the market is always the strongest lever for your success.

Starving Crowd Example: On the flip side, even if you are a terrible, unskilled entrepreneur, if you were selling toilet paper during COVID, you were making money.

Main Point: Your market matters.

So how do you pick the right market?

What I Look For In A Market

In order to sell anything, you need demand. We are not trying to *create* demand. We are trying to *channel* it. If you don't have a market for your offer, nothing that follows will work.

This entire book sits atop the assumption that you have at least a "normal" market, which I define as a market that is growing at the same rate as the marketplace.

That being said, having a great market is an advantage. But you can be in a normal market that's growing at an average rate and still make crazy money. Every market I have been in has been a normal market. You just don't *actually* want to be selling ice to eskimos.

Here are the four basic tenets of what I look for in markets:

1) Massive Pain

Pain can be anything that frustrates people about their lives. Being broke is painful. A bad marriage is painful. Waiting in line at the grocery stores is painful. Back pain . . . ugly smile pain . . . overweight pain . . . Humans suffer a lot. So for us entrepreneurs, endless opportunity abounds.

The degree of the pain will be proportional to the price you will be able to charge (more on this in the Value Equation chapter). When they hear the solution to their pain, and inversely, what their life would look like *without* this pain, they should be drawn to your solution.

A prospect must have a painful problem for us to solve and charge money for our solution.

2) Purchasing Power

A friend of mine had a very good system for helping people improve their resumes to get more job interviews. He was great at it. But try as he did, he just could not get people to pay for his services. Why? Because they were all unemployed!

This, again, may seem obvious. But he thought, *"These people are easy to target. They're in massive pain. There are plenty of them, and it's constantly adding new people. This is a great market!"*

He just forgot a crucial point: your audience needs to be able to afford the service you're charging them for. Make sure your targets have the money, or access to the amount of money, needed to buy your services at the prices you require to make it worth your time.

3) Easy to Target

You need to be able to target your ideal customers. For instance, you may *want* to serve rich doctors. But if your ads are being displayed to nursing students, your offer will fall on deaf ears, no matter how good it is.

<u>If I have to pick between two markets, I pick the one that's easier to advertise to.</u>

4) Growing

Growing markets are like a tailwind. They make everything move forward faster. Declining markets are like headwinds. They make all efforts harder. Find a market that's already growing, and you'll grow faster than you otherwise would just by participating in it.

Example: At the time of this writing, there are more people struggling with fertility than ever before. A business that solves this problem has a better chance than one that targets a shrinking market - like newspapers.

EXERCISE #3: What makes a market good to pursue?

Check off all variables that factor into picking a market.

- ☐ Technology
- ☐ Growth Rate
- ☐ Disposable Income
- ☐ Findability on platforms
- ☐ Need for the product
- ☐ Team
- ☐ Mindset

How important is this? Three Levers on Success

It's unlikely you are going to be in a dying market like the newspaper example. It's also unlikely you're going to be selling toilet paper in COVID (buying frenzy). You'll likely be in a "normal" market. And that's totally okay. There is a fortune to be made within normal markets. My single point here is that you can't be in a "bad" market, or nothing will work.

That being said, here's the simplest illustration of the order of importance between markets, offers, and persuasion skills:

Starving Crowd (market) > Offer Strength > Persuasion Skills

This idea is about three important things when selling something:

1) The people you sell to (market)

2) What you're selling (offer)

3) How good you are at convincing people (persuasion)

1. **If You're in a Great Market**: It's like selling snacks to a bunch of hungry people. Even if what you're selling isn't great and you're not the best at talking people into buying, you'll still probably sell a lot because the people really want what you have.

2. **Normal Market, but You Have a Great Thing to Sell**: If you're selling something really cool or useful, you can make a lot of money even if you're not the best at convincing people and the market is just okay.

3. **Normal Market and Normal Thing to Sell, but You're Great at Convincing People**: If you're really good at talking people into things, you can still do well, even if what you're selling and the people you're selling to are just average. But this way is harder and takes more work.

Bottom Line: It's best to find a really good market first, then make sure what you're selling is great, and also be good at convincing people to buy it. Each part is important, but some are more important than others.

> ### EXERCISE #4: What matters most?
>
> Rank the following in order of importance from 1 to 3.
> _____ Marketing and Sales ability
> _____ Offer Strength
> _____ Supply - Demand

HOW TO MAKE A GRAND SLAM OFFER

Once You Pick Your Niche, Commit to It

Too often, a newer entrepreneur half-heartedly tries *one* offer in *one* market, doesn't make a million dollars, then mistakenly thinks "this is a bad market." Most times that's not actually the case. They just haven't found a Grand Slam Offer yet to apply to that market.

They think, *I'll switch from helping dentists to helping chiropractors — that's it!* When, in reality, both of those are normal markets and represent billions of dollars in revenue. Either would work, *just not both*. You must pick *one*. So, pick then commit.

Riches Are In The Niches

The other reason to commit to the niche is because of how much more you will make. Simply put, niching down will make you far more money.

> **Author Note:** If you are already at $10M+ per year in revenue, you may be better off going wider or into an adjacent market. This niche advice is particularly important for those under $10,000,000 per year in revenue.

Reason: you can literally charge 100x more for the *exact* same product. Let me illustrate:

Niching Product Pricing Example:

Example

Product	Price
Time Management	$19
Time Management For Sales Professionals	$99
Time Management For Outbound B2B Sales	$499
Time Management For Outbound B2B Power Tools & Gardening Sales Reps	$1997

20   Copyright © 2024 by ACQUISITION.COM LLC NOT FOR DISTRIBUTION

Dan Kennedy uses this example to teach the power of niche pricing. All four of these are more or less identical products. But, by picking the right person to market it to, you can charge 100x more money for the same thing. At each level, we become more specific, and our pricing reflects this increased level of personalization.

EXERCISE #5: Pick Your Niche, 4 levels deep.

State your current product: . . . .
Add one category focus: . . . .
Add subcategory: . . . .
Re-write new niche: . . . .

Summary:

The purpose of this chapter is to reinforce <u>three</u> things:

- **First**, don't pick a *bad* market. Normal markets are fine. Great markets are great.

- **Second**, once you pick, commit to it until you figure it out.

- **Third**, if you are starting out, be specific about who you want to serve. Narrow is okay. It allows you to charge more for the same thing to get more cash flow to figure out what you're doing.

FREE GIFT #2 BONUS TUTORIAL: WINNING MARKETS

If you want to know more about how I pick markets, and find niches that are profitable, go to **Acquisition.com/ training/offers** course then watch "Winning Markets" for a short video tutorial. I've also included a Free Checklist to see how your market or niche measures up. You can also scan the QR Code if you don't like typing. It's absolutely free. Enjoy.

Problem #3: You Price Too Low To Make Money
→ Solution #3: Premium Pricing

"Charge as high a price as you can say out loud without cracking a smile."
— **Dan Kennedy**

A picture of Gym Lords Summit 2019 for our highest level gym owners all sporting my trendy mustache.

Every person in the picture above paid $42,000 to be in the room. I showed my dad the picture and he asked if *they* knew that. Of course they did. He just couldn't imagine ever paying for something like that. In other words, he understood the PRICE but he couldn't understand the VALUE.

The reason people buy *anything* is to get a *deal*. They believe what they are getting (VALUE) is worth *more* than what they are giving in exchange for it (PRICE). The moment the value they receive dips below what they are paying, they stop buying from you. A shrinking price to value discrepancy is what you need to avoid at all costs.

After all, as Warren Buffet said, "Price is what you pay. Value is what you get."

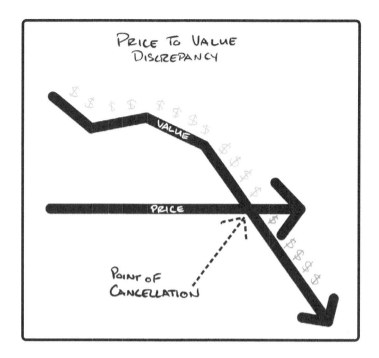

1) The simplest way to increase the gap between price to value is by lowering the price. It's also, most of the time, the wrong decision for the business.

2) The other way is to increase your value. This way, customers still get a great deal (think buying $100,000 of value for $10,000). It's 'money at a discount.'

As Dan Kennedy said, "There is no strategic benefit to being the second cheapest in the marketplace, but there is for being the most expensive."

Let me show you why…

EXERCISE #6: Price to Value Discrepancy

To expand price to value discrepancy, check off some appropriate actions:

☐ Offer discounts
☐ Lower price
☐ Add Guarantee
☐ Add Features/Services
☐ Provide faster delivery

Virtuous Cycle of Price

Here's the basic premise of why you *need* to charge a premium if you want to best serve your customers.

When you decrease your price, you . . .

. . . Decrease your clients' emotional investment since it didn't cost them much

. . . Decrease your clients' perceived value of your service since it can't be that good if it's so cheap, or priced the same as everyone else

. . . Decrease your clients' results because they do not value your service and are not invested

. . . Attract the worst clients who are *never* satisfied until your service is *free*

. . . Destroy any margin you have left to be able to actually provide an exceptional experience, hire the best people, invest in your people, pamper your clients, invest in growth, invest in more locations or more scale, and everything else that you had hoped in the goal of helping more people solve whatever problem it is that you solve.

In essence, your world sucks.

Here's the reverse. This is what happens when you raise your prices.

When you raise your prices, you . . .

. . . *Increase* your clients' emotional investment

. . . *Increase* your clients' perceived value of your service

. . . *Increase* your clients' results because they value your service and are invested

. . . Attract the *best* clients who are *the easiest* to satisfy and actually cost *less* to fulfill, and who are the most likely to actually receive and perceive the most relative value

. . . *Multiply* your margin because you have money to *invest* in systems to create efficiency; smart people; improved customer experience; scale your business; and, most importantly of all, to keep watching the number in your personal bank account go up, month after month, even with reinvesting in your business. This allows you to ultimately enjoy the process for the long haul and help more people as you grow, rather than burning out and shriveling into obscurity.

To swing the argument even further in favor of higher prices, here are a few interesting concepts. When you raise your price, you increase the value the consumer receives without changing anything else about your product. Wait, what? Yes.

EXERCISE #7: Increased Prices

Which of the following happen when you raise prices?

- ☐ Sell more customers
- ☐ Sell better customers
- ☐ Get people better results
- ☐ Lower emotional investment from customers
- ☐ Make more profit
- ☐ Outspend your competition
- ☐ Harder to attract talented employees

Higher Price Means Higher Value (Literally)

Study: They had people taste three wines with the prices showing. A cheap, medium, and expensive bottle. People rated them in order of the price. What they didn't know is all three were the same wine.

This means that price actually increases the *perceived value* of what you sell. So you can, in a real way, make people perceive your thing as more valuable simply by raising the price. What's more, the higher the price, the more allure your product or service has. People *want* to buy expensive things. They just need a reason. And the goal isn't just to be slightly above the market price — the goal is to be so much higher that a consumer thinks to themselves, "This is so much more expensive, there must be something entirely different going on here."

That is how you create a category of one. In this new perceived marketplace, you are a monopoly and can make monopoly profits. That is the point.

Also - if you have a service where the customer needs to do something in order to be successful - charging more increases people's emotional investment. So if you want to have a higher success percentage, raise your prices.

Summary Points

1) Charge a premium price because:

    a) No one wins in a race to the bottom

    b) You can use the extra profits to make your thing better than everyone else's

    c) You get better customers

    d) You attract better talent

    e) You are more convicted

    f) They get more emotionally bought in

    g) They'll automatically perceive you as higher value (wine example)

2) Don't be afraid.

FREE GIFT #3: BONUS TUTORIAL & FREE DOWNLOADS:
Charge What It's Worth

If you want to know how I create value discrepancies for B2B or B2C products, go to **Acquisition.com/training/offers** course then watch **"Charge What It's Worth"** for a short video tutorial. My goal is to gain your trust and deliver value in advance. You can also scan the QR Code if you don't like typing. As such, it's absolutely free. Enjoy.

SCAN ME

Problem #4: Your Thing Isn't Valuable
→ Solution #4: Make It Valuable

Value Offer: The Value Equation

> *"We question all of our beliefs, except for the ones we really believe in, and those we never think to question."*
> — **Orson Scott Card**

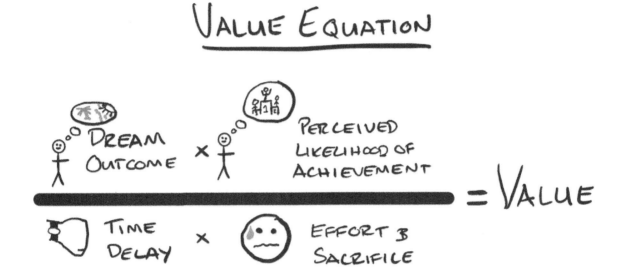

To charge lots of money, you need to provide even more value. The equation above shows the relationship between the four value drivers.

Two of the drivers (on top), you want to increase. The other two (on the bottom), you want to decrease.

(1) (Yay) The Dream Outcome (Goal: Increase)

(2) (Yay) Perceived Likelihood of Achievement (Goal: Increase)

(3) (Boo) Perceived Time Delay Between Start and Achievement (Goal: Decrease)

(4) (Boo) Perceived Effort & Sacrifice (Goal: Decrease)

These value drivers typically correspond with the questions you will hear from a prospect when they are trying to figure out if your offer is "worth it":

What will I make? <u>and/or</u> *What will happen?* (Dream Outcome)

How will I know it's going to happen? (Perceived Likelihood of Achievement)

How long will it take? (Time Delay)

What is expected of me? (Effort & Sacrifice)

Get The Bottom To Zero

Newbies focus on promising bigger and showing more testimonials.

Pros focus on making things effortless and immediate.

Reason: No matter how small the top side is, anything divided by zero equals infinity (which is technically undefined for the math nerds). In other words, if you can reduce your prospects' true time delay to receiving value to zero (aka you realize your immediate dream outcome), and your effort and sacrifice is zero, you have an infinitely valuable product. If you accomplish this, you win the game.

Given this concept, a prospect would (in theory) purchase something from you, and the moment their credit card was run, it would immediately become their reality. *That* is infinite value.

Imagine clicking the purchase button on a weight loss product and instantly seeing your stomach turn into a six-pack. Or imagine hiring a marketing firm, and as soon as you sign your document, your phone begins ringing with new highly qualified prospects. How valuable would these products/services be? Infinitely valuable. And that's the point.

EXERCISE #8: Which of the following apply to "getting the bottom to zero"?

☐ Faster customer support response times
☐ Saved credit card at checkout
☐ Testimonials
☐ Guarantees
☐ Surprise next day shipping
☐ Pre-filled out forms
☐ Immediate and personalized onboarding

Perception is Reality

For all value drivers, it's not about what you think they are, or about what they are, but about what your prospect *thinks* they are. So you need to communicate the value drivers in language they can understand so they can *perceive* the value.

Example: London Tunnel System

The biggest increase in rider satisfaction (*aka value*) was never from faster trains to decrease wait times. Instead, it was from a simple dotted map that showed them when the next train was coming and how long they had to wait. The dotted map, which only cost a few million dollars, decreased the riders' *perception* of time delay and sacrifice (being bored waiting) more than actually making the trains faster (which costs billions of dollars to do). Isn't that cool? This is how we need to think about our products.

Logical Vs Psychological Solutions

Most people try and solve problems using *logical* solutions. But the logical solutions have usually been tried...because they're logical (it's what everyone would try and do). As a business owner and entrepreneur I increasingly approach problems to find *psychological* solutions, rather than *logical* ones. Because if there were a logical solution, it probably would have already been solved, thereby eliminating the problem. All that's left are the *psychological* problems.

Examples inspired by Rory Sutherland, CMO of Ogilvy Advertising:

"Any fool can sell a product by offering it for a discount, it takes great marketing to sell the same product for a premium"

Trains

- Logical solution: make trains faster to increase satisfaction

- Psychological solution: decrease the pain of waiting by adding a dotted map

- Psychological solution: pay models to be the hostesses on the trip (people would wish it took longer to get to their destination!)

Elevators

- Logical solution: make elevator faster

- Psychological solution: add floor to ceiling mirrors so people are distracted staring at themselves and forget how long they were on the elevator

Pricing

- Logical solution: make it cheaper

- Psychological solution: make fewer of them and raise the price which causes people to want it more.

Often, most logical solutions have been tried and failed. At this point in history, we must give the psychological solutions a shot to solve problems.

#1 Dream Outcome (Goal = Increase)

The dream outcome is the thing they want. Often it's:

. . . To be perceived as beautiful

. . . To be respected

. . . To be perceived as powerful

. . . To be loved

. . . To increase their *status*

These are all powerful drivers.

Note, different offers may attempt to accomplish the same dream outcome. Take the desire *"to be perceived as beautiful"* for example, here are a lot of things that touch on this desire:

Makeup

Anti-aging creams/serums

Supplements

Shapewear

Plastic Surgery

Fitness

→ All these vehicles channel the desire to *be perceived as beautiful.*

Oftentimes, dream outcomes at their core reflect an increase in social standing (status) within one's group.

Two Offers, Different Dream Outcomes: The dream outcome value driver is most prominently used when comparing the relative value *between two different desires being satisfied.*

Different Dream Outcome Example: For many men, making money is more important than getting in shape. Main reason: making money increases their status with men and women more than getting in shape will. This would mean, as a category, men who feel this way will likely put a premium on offers that help achieve the "make money" dream outcome more than the "get in shape" dream outcome.

Two Offers, Same Dream Outcome: When comparing two products or services that satisfy the *same* desire, the value from the dream outcomes will cancel out (since they are the same). It will be the other three variables that drive the difference in perceived value, and ultimately price.

Same Dream Outcome Example: if we have two products or services that both help make someone beautiful, it will be the likelihood of achievement, time delay, and effort required that will differentiate the perceived value of each offer.

Simply put: if two things make someone beautiful, what makes one worth $50,000 and another $5? Answer: The extent of the other three value variables.

#2 Perceived Likelihood of Achievement (Goal = Increase)

People value certainty. They pay a premium for it. I call this "the perceived likelihood of achievement." In other words, "How likely do I believe it is that I will achieve the result I am looking for if I make this purchase?" In other words, the opposite of *risk*.

Example: How much would you pay to be a plastic surgeon's 10,000th patient versus their first? Answer: A lot more. Why? Because even though they are technically the same procedure, your perceived likelihood of achievement is much higher. And you're willing to pay a premium for it to *decrease your risk*.

Bottom line: Increasing a prospect's conviction that your offer will "actually" work for them, makes your offer more valuable even though you do the same work. You communicate perceived likelihood of achievement through: social proof (think testimonials), guarantees (think if you don't get x, I'll give you y), and third party authority (think degrees).

EXERCISE #9: Increasing certainty & lowering risk

Check off all that apply:

- ☐ Telling your story of achievement and relating it to theirs
- ☐ Testimonials
- ☐ 5-Star Reviews
- ☐ Certifications/Degrees/Third party accreditations
- ☐ Numbers, stats, research that supports the outcome you want them to believe
- ☐ Experts vouching for us
- ☐ Unique characteristic that explains why they failed before
- ☐ Celebrities endorsements
- ☐ Guarantees
- ☐ Live demonstrations prior to purchase

#3 Time Delay (Goal = Decrease)

Time delay *is the time between a client buying and receiving the promised benefit.* The short-er the distance between when they purchase and when they receive value/the outcome, the more valuable your services or product is. In other words, *speed*.

Time Delay Example: It's the reason people will pay $25,000 for immediate results with liposuction, while people will barely pay $29/mo for a gym membership to wait 12 to 24 months for results. 12 to 24 months to get what you want is a *long* time when you can do liposuction and be done in an afternoon. Same outcome. Different speeds. Wildly different prices people are willing to pay.

There are two elements to this driver:

1. Long-term outcome - how long it takes for them to get to their destination

2. Short-term experience - how long it takes them to experience *some* benefit

Ideally: create an emotional win as fast as possible. This is even more important if you sell a result that takes a long time for them to experience. You want to break up some "smaller win" you can deliver sooner.

Short Team Experience Example: If I sell someone a bikini body, their time delay to realize that outcome may be 12 months or even longer. Along the way, though, as they change their bodies, they may experience higher sex drive, more energy, and an increased community of friends.

They aren't *initially* buying those things, but those things may become short-term benefits that keep them in the game long enough to achieve their ultimate outcome.

This is also backed by science. People who experience a victory early on are more likely to continue with something than those who do not.

Using our liposuction versus gym membership example, speed is one element that makes up the dramatic price difference. But there's also another: effort & sacrifice.

Pro Tip: Fast Beats Free

The only thing that beats "free" is "fast." People will pay for speed. Many companies have entered free spaces and done exceedingly well with a "speed first" strategy. A few notable examples: The MVD vs DMV wait in line forever or pay $50 you can skip the line and get your license renewed privately. Fedex vs USPS (when it absolutely positively has to be there overnight). Spotify vs Slow Free Music. Uber vs Walking. Fast beats free. Many will always be willing to pay (price) for the (value) of speed. So if you find yourself in a market competing against free, double down on speed.

EXERCISE #10: Speed

Break down all the micro events that happen in your customer journey.

. . . .

. . . .

. . . .

. . . .

. . . .

. . . .

Write down how long it takes for you to do them.

. . . .

. . . .

Next, see how you can deliver them in 1/3 the time if you had to.

#4 Effort & Sacrifice (Goal = Decrease)

This is what it "costs" people in ancillary costs, aka "other costs accrued along the way." These can be both tangible and intangible.

Effort is *what you have to start doing (that you dislike) as a result of the purchase.*

Sacrifice is *what you have to give up (that you like) as a result of the purchase.*

They are equal sides of the same coin. Using the fitness versus liposuction example, let's look at the difference in effort and sacrifice:

Fitness Effort and Sacrifice:	Liposuction effort and sacrifice:
Wake up one to two hours earlier in the morning	Fall asleep
Five to ten hours per week of time lost	Wake up thin, guaranteed
Stop eating the foods you love	Be sore for two to four weeks
Constant hunger	
Physical soreness	
Feelings of embarrassment at not knowing how to exercise	
Risk of injury	
Actual nausea working out	
Meal prepping	
New groceries/more expensive	
New clothing (can be a benefit for some folks)	
Fear of gaining it back after all this effort (impermanence)	
Etc . . .	

See the difference?

If you don't, look at the marketing of plastic surgeons. These are the *exact* pain points they hit on when they say things like: *"Tired of wasting countless hours in the gym. . . . tired of trying diets that just don't work?"*

There's just not a lot of perceived value in fitness because the perceived likelihood of achievement, the time delay to achievement, and the effort and sacrifice are so high.

The goal is to keep these as low as possible - and in so doing - make your thing far more valuable.

EXERCISE #11: Increase Ease, Decrease Effort

List all the things your customer has to give up to use your stuff.

. . . .

. . . .

. . . .

. . . .

. . . .

. . . .

List all the things your customer has to start doing to use your stuff.

. . . .

. . . .

. . . .

. . . .

. . . .

. . . .

See how you can preserve as many from list A.

See how you can eliminate or "take care of" as many as possible from list B for them.

Putting It All Together

These elements of value don't happen in a vacuum. They happen together, in combination. So let's look at a few examples that utilize all four components of value at once.

To quantify the value, I'll rate them on a binary scale of 0 or 1. 1 being value achieved. 0 being missing. Then I will add all four together to give you a relative value rating of a type of service.

Reminder: the goal is to *increase the dream outcome* and *the perceived likelihood of achievement* while *decreasing* the *time delay and effort*.

Example: Let's do a side by side comparison using the value equation of two offers with identical Dream outcomes: Meditation and Xanax. Both offer the buyer relaxation, decreased anxiety, and feelings of well-being.

Value Measure	Meditation	Score	Xanax	Score
Dream Outcome	"Relaxation" "Decreased Anxiety" "Feelings of well-being"	1/1	"Relaxation" "Decreased Anxiety" "Feelings of well-being"	1/1
Perceived Likelihood	Low, since most people get distracted and don't actually think they'll follow through with daily meditation	0/1	High, since most people are confident that if they take the pill, it will make them feel more relaxed	1/1
Time Delay	Long time to yield long term results. Some immediate benefits after 10 to 20 minutes (assuming you don't get frustrated)	.5/1	15 minutes for effects to be felt	1/1
Effort & Sacrifice	Physical discomfort (numb body limbs often). Mental discomfort (feeling like you are failing at it constantly). Time sacrifice (you have to set time aside everyday to do it).	0/1	Swallowing the pill	1/1
Overall Value	**Low**	1.5/4	**High**	4/4

EXERCISE #12: Rate Your Current Offer

1) Dream Outcome: (0 / 1)

2) Perceived Likelihood: (0 / 1)

3) Time Delay: (0 / 1)

4) Ease/Effort & Sacrifice: (0 / 1)

5) Total Value out of 4: . . . .

And that is why Xanax is a multi-billion dollar product while I know of almost no multi-billion dollar meditation businesses . . . value.

And you can either sit there and make "complain" posts about how people "ought" to be a certain way. Or you can take advantage of the way people *are* and capitalize.

This book is for getting rich. If that bothers you, just put this down and go back to arguing against human nature. Hint: You're not gonna change it.

FREE GIFT #4: Value Equation Bonus Tutorial & Free Download(s):

If you want to know how I break down a business's core offering into something more valuable go to **Acquisition.com/training/offers** and select the **"Value Equation"** video to watch a short tutorial. I also included a downloadable checklist. My goal is to *gain your trust* and deliver value in advance. You can also scan the QR Code if you don't like typing. As such, it's absolutely free. Enjoy.

FREE GOODWILL

"He who said money can't buy happiness, hasn't given enough away."
— Unknown

People who help others (with zero expectation) experience higher levels of fulfillment, live longer, *and* make more money. I'd like to create the opportunity to deliver this value to you during your reading or listening experience. In order to do so, I have a simple question for you...

Would you help someone you've never met, if it didn't cost you money, but you never got credit for it?

If so, I have an 'ask' to make on behalf of someone you do not know. And likely, never will.

They are just like you, or like you were a few years ago: less experienced, full of desire to help the world, seeking information but unsure where to look....this is where you come in.

The only way for us at Acquisition.com to accomplish our mission of helping entrepreneurs is, first, by reaching them. And most people do, in fact, judge a book by its cover (and its reviews). If you have found this book valuable thus far, would you please take a brief moment right now and leave an honest review of the book and its contents? It will cost you zero dollars and less than 60 seconds.

Your review will help....

....one more entrepreneur supports his or her family.

....one more employee finds work they find meaningful.

....one more client experience a transformation they otherwise would never have encountered.

....one more life change for the better.

To make that happen...all you have to do is....and this takes less than 60 seconds.... leave a review.

If you are on audible - hit the three dots in the top right of your device, click rate & review, then leave a few sentences about the book with a star rating.

<u>If you are reading on Kindle or an e-reader</u> - you can scroll to the bottom of the book, then swipe up and it will automatically prompt a review.

<u>If for some reason they have changed either functionality</u> - you can go to the book page on Amazon (or wherever you purchased this) and leave a review right on the page.

PS - If you feel good about helping a faceless entrepreneur, you are my kind of people. I'm that much more excited to help you crush it in the coming chapters (you'll love the tactics I'm about to go over).

PPS - Life hack: if you introduce something valuable to someone, they associate that value with you. If you'd like goodwill directly from another entrepreneur - send this book their way.

Thank you from the bottom of my heart. Now back to our regularly scheduled programming.

- Your biggest fan, Alex

EXERCISE #13: If this workbook has provided value in excess of its cost, please leave it a review :)

Problem #5: You're Solving The Wrong Way
→ Solution #5: Solve The Right Way

"If at first you don't succeed, try, try, try again."
— **Thomas H. Palmer, Teacher's Manual**

I want to show you the difference between convergent and divergent problem solving. Why? So that you can actually create the Grand Slam Offer that will become the cornerstone of your business.

Convergent & Divergent Thinking

In simple terms, convergent problem solving is where you take lots of variables, all known, with unchanging conditions and converge on a singular answer. Think math.

Example:

You have 3 salespeople who can each take 100 calls per month each.

It takes 4 calls to create one sale (including no shows).

You need to get to 110 sales . . .

How many salespeople must you hire?

Deduced Information:

1 salesperson = 100 calls

4 calls = 1 close

100 calls/4 calls per close = 25 Closes Per 100 Calls

25 closes per rep

Goal: 110 sales *total* / 25 sales per rep = 4.4

Since you can't hire 4.4 reps, you decide you must have *five*.

ANSWER: And since you have 3, you hire *two* more.

Math problems are convergent. There are lots of variables and a single answer. We are taught all our lives in school to think this way. <u>That is because it's easy to grade.</u>

But life will pay you for your ability to solve using a divergent thought process. In other words, think of many solutions to a single problem. Not only that, convergent answers are binary. They are either right or they are wrong. With divergent thinking, you can have multiple right answers, and one answer that is way more right than the others. Cool right?

Here's what life presents us for divergent thinking: Multiple Variables, Known & Unknown, Dynamic Conditions, Multiple Answers.

As such, I want to do an exercise with you that will engage the part of your brain that you will need to use in order to make something magical.

I call it the "brick" exercise. Don't worry, it'll only take 120 seconds.

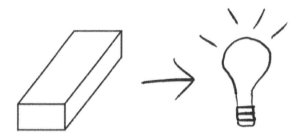

EXERCISE #14: The Brick Exercise

Right now, I want you to set a timer on your phone for 120 seconds. What you need to do: Think of a brick.

Write down as many *different* uses of a brick as you can possibly think of. How many different ways could a brick be used in life to provide value.

Ready? Go. It's okay to write in the book.

Alright — stop. Now before I show you my list, did you consider the following . . .

. . . How big is the brick? A tab of gum, 3-5/8" x 2-1/4" x 8" (Standard), 2 ft x 2 ft x 6ft?

. . . What is the brick made of? Plastic, Gold, Clay, Wood, Metal?

. . . How is the brick shaped? Does it have holes in it? Does it have divots for interlocking?

Now as you think about that, can you think of even more uses for the brick than you probably wrote down?

Here's my list:

— Paperweight

— Doorstop

— Building things

— Home for a fish in a fish bowl

— Plant holder with dirt in the holes (holed brick)

— As a trophy (painted brick)

— Rustic decoration

— To break window

— Make a mural (tiny bricks painted)

— A weight for resistance training

— A wedge under an uneven platform

— Pen holder (holed brick)

— Children's toy (lego bricks)

— Floatation device (plastic brick)

— Payment for goods (gold brick)

— Stabilizer for leaning something against

— Holder for flagpole (holed brick)

— A seat (jumbo brick)

Every offer has building blocks, the pieces that when combined make an offer irresistible. Our goal is to use a divergent thought process to think of as many easy ways to combine these elements to provide value.

So if I were selling a brick, I would find out what my customer's desire was, and then devise how many ways I could create value with my "brick." Now let's do it for real.

Problem #6: You're Solving The Wrong Problems → Solution #6: Solve the Right Problems

"ABC, Easy as 123 Ah, simple as do re mi"
— **Michael Jackson, "ABC"**

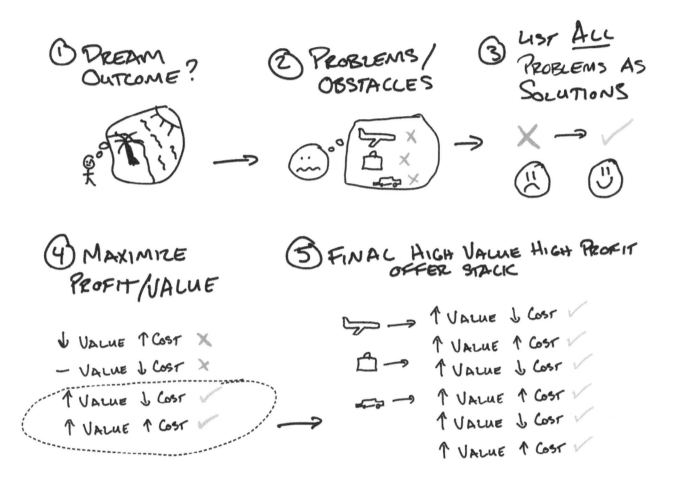

Here's how you make an offer so good people feel stupid saying no. In other words, a grand slam offer.

EXERCISE #15 (Offer Step 1): Identify Dream Outcome

Clearly state what the person wants to achieve within a specific timeframe.

Example: I had heard of weight loss challenges, so I started there. Lose 20lbs in 6 weeks. Big dream outcome - lose 20lbs. With a decreased time delay - 6 weeks.

Note: I wasn't selling my membership anymore. I wasn't selling the plane flight. *I was selling the vacation.* When you are thinking about your dream outcome, it has to be them arriving at their destination and what they would like to *experience.*

Dream Outcome: . . . .
. . . .

Timeframe: . . . .

EXERCISE #16 (Offer Step 2): List Problems

Next, write down all the things people struggle with and their limiting thoughts around them.

Tip: Think about what happens immediately before and immediately after someone uses your product/service. Get very detailed.

Example Problem List: Weight Loss

First thing they must do: Buying healthy food, grocery shopping

1) Buying healthy food is hard, confusing, and I won't like it
2) Buying healthy food will take too much time
3) Buying healthy food is expensive
4) I will not be able to cook healthy food forever. My family's needs will get in my way. If I travel I won't know what to get.

Next thing they must do: *Cooking healthy food*

1) Cooking healthy food is hard and confusing. I won't like it, and I will suck at it.
2) Cooking healthy food will take too much time
3) Cooking healthy food is expensive. It's not worth it.
4) I will not be able to buy healthy food forever. My family's needs will get in my way. If I travel I won't know how to cook healthy.

Next thing they must do: *Eating healthy food*

1)   Etc...

Next thing they must do: *Exercise Regularly*

1)   Etc...

Now we're gonna go full circle here. Each of the above problems has four negative elements. And you guessed it, each aligns with the four value drivers as well.

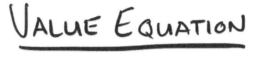

Now, go ahead and list out all the problems your prospect has.

The more problems you think of, the more problems you get to solve.

Work through each problem you can think of, then think of it through the four value drivers.

How do I make this a better outcome?

. . . .
. . . .
. . . .

How do I make it less risky?

. . . .
. . . .
. . . .

How do I make this faster?

....

....

....

How do I make this easier?

....

....

....

EXERCISE #17 (Offer Step 3): Solutions List

Go back to your problems list above. Label each problem with a number. Write as many numbers below as you have problems above. Now write "how to" next to each number and turn the problem into solution oriented language. Examples below.

How do I make this a better outcome? <u>Rewrite the problem as a "how to" solution.</u>

....

....

....

How do I make it less risky? <u>Rewrite the problem as a "how to" solution.</u>

....

....

....

How do I make this faster? <u>Rewrite the problem as a "how to" solution.</u>

....

....

....

How do I make this easier? <u>Rewrite the problem as a "how to" solution.</u>

....

....

....

Example:

PROBLEM: Buying healthy food, grocery shopping

. . . is hard, confusing, I won't like it. I will suck at it→ How to make buying healthy food easy and enjoyable, so that anyone can do it (especially busy moms!)

. . . takes too much time→ How to buy healthy food quickly

. . . is expensive→ How to buy healthy food for less than your current grocery bill

. . . is unsustainable→ How to make buying healthy food take less effort than buying unhealthy food

. . . is not my priority. My family's needs will get in my way→ How to buy healthy food for you and your family at the same time

. . . is undoable if I travel; I won't know what to get→ How to get healthy food when traveling

PROBLEM: Eating healthy food

. . . is hard, confusing, and I won't like it→ How to eat delicious healthy food, without following complicated systems

. . . etc.

PROBLEM: Exercise Regularly

. . . is hard, confusing, and I won't like it, and I will suck at it → Easy to follow exercise system that everyone enjoys

. . . .etc.

Note: It's okay if your solutions sound repetitive. People still make decisions around the four core drivers. And - if you're missing even one solution to a problem - a percentage of people won't buy. So you wanna solve 'em all!

EXERCISE #18 (Offer Step 4): Create Your Solutions Delivery Vehicles ("The How")

Now we have to actually turn these "headlines" of solutions into actual activities we're going to do. This is where promises meet fulfillment.

That being said, if this is your first Grand Slam Offer, it's important to over-deliver like crazy. Everyone buys bargains. Some people just buy $100,000 things for only $10,000. That's where we want to live: high prices, but a *steal* for the value (like hopefully this workbook so far).

Let me introduce you to the sales to fulfillment continuum.

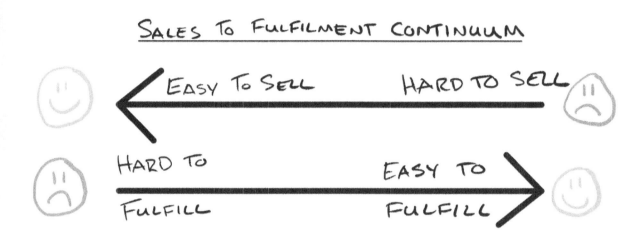

Whenever you are building a business, you have a continuum between ease of fulfillment and ease of sales. If you lower what you have to do, it increases how hard your product or service is to sell. If you do as much as possible, it makes your product or service easy to sell but hard to fulfill because there's more demand on your time investment. The trick, and the ultimate goal, is to find a sweet spot where you sell something very well that's also easy to fulfill.

Now that you have this mental reframe, the next step is thinking about all the things you could *do* to solve each of these problems you've identified. **This is the most important step in this process.**

For now, write down *anything you could possibly do* to solve the problem. Seriously. Anything. Doing this exercise will make your job of selling So. Much. Easier.

Reminder: You only need to do this *once*. Literally *one time* for a product that may last years. This is high-value, high-leverage work. The goal is to be creative and push your mental limits. Go ahead. List out all potential solutions that you could offer to solve these problems. Don't worry about scaling it yet. We'll get to that.

Examples:

Problem: Buying Healthy Food Is Hard, Confusing, and I Won't Like It

If I wanted to provide a one-on-one solution I might offer . . .

a) In-person grocery shopping, where I take clients to the store and teach them how to shop
b) Personalized grocery list, where I teach them how to make their list
c) Full-service shopping, where I buy their food for them. We're talking 100 percent done for them.
d) In-person orientation (not at store), where I teach them what to get
e) Text support while shopping, where I help them if they get stuck
f) Phone call while grocery shopping, where I plan to call when they go shopping to provide direction and support

If I wanted to provide a small group solution I might offer . . .

a) In-person grocery shopping, where I meet a bunch of people and take them all shopping for themselves
b) Personalized grocery list, where I teach a bunch of people how to make their weekly lists. I could do this one time or every week if I wanted to.
c) Buy their food for them, where I purchase their groceries and deliver them as well
d) In-person orientation, where I teach a small group offsite what to do (not at store)

If I wanted to provide a one to many solution I might offer . . .

a) Live grocery tour virtual, where I might live stream me going through the grocery store for all my new customers and let them ask questions live
b) Recorded grocery tour, where I might shop once, record it, then give it as a reference point from that point onwards for my clients to watch on their own
c) DIY grocery calculator, where I create a shareable tool or show them how to use a tool to calculate their grocery list
d) Predetermined lists, where each customer plan comes with its own grocery list for each week. I could make this ahead of time so they have it. Then they could use it on their own time

e) Grocery buddy system, where I could pair customers all up, which takes no time really, and let them go shopping together

f) Pre-made, insta-cart grocery carts for delivery, where I could pre-make insta-cart lists so clients could have their groceries delivered to their doorstep with one click

The list can really go on and on here. This is just to illustrate the many ways to solve a *single* problem.

Action Step: Do this for *all* of the perceived problems that your clients encounter before, after, and during their experience with your service/products. You should have a monster list by the end of this.

Potential Solution for Problem #1. . . . .

Potential Solution for Problem #1. . . . .

Potential Solution for Problem #1. . . . .

Potential Solution for Problem #1. . . . .

Potential Solution for Problem #1. . . . .

Potential Solution for Problem #1. . . . .

Potential Solution for Problem #2. . . . .

Potential Solution for Problem #2. . . . .

Potential Solution for Problem #2. . . . .

Potential Solution for Problem #2. . . . .

Potential Solution for Problem #2. . . . .

Potential Solution for Problem #2. . . . .

Potential Solution for Problem #3. . . . .

Potential Solution for Problem #3. . . . .

Potential Solution for Problem #3. . . . .

Potential Solution for Problem #3. . . . .

Potential Solution for Problem #3. . . . .

Potential Solution for Problem #3. . . . .

Potential Solution for Problem #4. . . . .

Potential Solution for Problem #4. . . . .

Potential Solution for Problem #4. . . . .

Potential Solution for Problem #4. . . . .

Potential Solution for Problem #4. . . . .

Potential Solution for Problem #5. . . . .

Potential Solution for Problem #5. . . . .

Potential Solution for Problem #5. . . . .

Potential Solution for Problem #5. . . . .

Potential Solution for Problem #5. . . . .

Potential Solution for Problem #5. . . . .

Potential Solution for Problem #6. . . . .

Potential Solution for Problem #6. . . . .

Potential Solution for Problem #6. . . . .

Potential Solution for Problem #6. . . . .

Potential Solution for Problem #6. . . . .

Potential Solution for Problem #6. . . . .

Keep going until done

Product Delivery Cheat Codes

If you're struggling, this is a mental framework I call the "Delivery Cube."

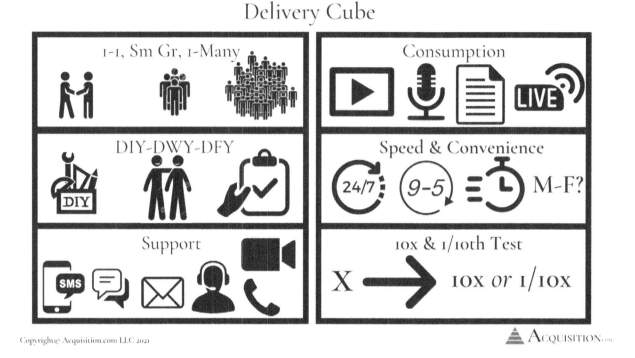

It helps me think through each element of *value delivery*. Let's walk through them together.

a) TOP LEFT: What level of personal attention do I want to provide? one-on-one, small group, one to many

b) MIDDLE LEFT: What level of effort is expected from them? Do it themselves (DIY) - figure out how to do it on their own; do it with them (DWY) - you teach them how to do it; done for them (DFY) - you do it for them

c) BOTTOM LEFT: If doing something live, what environment or medium do I want to deliver it in? In-person, phone support, email support, text support, Zoom support, chat support

d) TOP RIGHT: If doing a recording, how do I want them to consume it? Audio, video, or written.

e) MIDDLE RIGHT: How quickly do we want to reply? On what days? During what hours? 24/7. 9-5, within 5 minutes, within an hour, within 24 hrs?

f) <u>BOTTOM RIGHT: 10x to 1/10th test.</u> If my customers paid me 10x my price (or $100,000) what would I provide? If they paid me 1/10th the price and I had to make my product more valuable than it already is, how would I do that? How could I still make them successful for 1/10th price? Stretch your mind in either direction and you'll come up with widely different solutions.

In other words, how could I actually *deliver* on these solutions I am claiming I will provide.

Action Step: Do this for <u>every</u> problem because solutions from one problem will give you ideas for others you wouldn't normally have considered.

Author note: I can't tell you the amount of times *one* single item becomes the reason someone doesn't buy. Solve them all.

Example: I used to sell weight loss. One time, after an hour of talking, I had a lady who wouldn't buy it because she traveled a lot. I asked her if she would buy it if I made a plan for when she traveled. She immediately said yes. Find out why people aren't buying. Solve that. Then include it going forward.

EXERCISE #19 (Offer Step 5a): Trim & Stack

You should now have a gigantic list of things you *could* do to solve *all* their problems. Now, we need to make our offer profitable.

Action step: Go back to your list above. Write the cost of providing these solutions to the business in the margin (keep it simple with: "**H**igh, **M**ed, **L**ow"). Now go back to the list and guess the relative value (use the same "**H, M, L**" ratings). Cross out the ones that are high cost and low value first. Then remove low cost, low value items.

What should remain are offer items that are 1) low cost, high value and 2) high cost, high value.

Weight loss example: Let's say I moved in with someone and did their shopping, exercising, and cooking for them. They would probably believe they would definitely lose weight. But I am not willing to do that for any amount of money short of a gazillion dollars.

The next question becomes, is there a lesser version of this experience that I can deliver at scale?

Just take one step back at a time until you arrive at something that has a time commitment or cost you are willing to live with (or, obviously, massively increase your price so it becomes worth it for you — i.e., the gazillion dollars to live with someone).

What to focus on: Creating high value, "one to many" solutions. These will be the ones that typically have the biggest discrepancy between cost and value.

Low Cost High Value Example: Before I started my first gym, I had an online training business. I created a small spreadsheet that after inputting all of someone's goals, automatically generated over 100 meals perfectly suited to their macronutrient and calorie needs. It would tell them what they needed to buy at the grocery store in exact amounts, *and* how to prepare them in bulk for their exact amounts.

It took me about 100 hours to put the whole thing together. But from that point going forward I sold truly personalized eating plans for very expensive prices, but they only took me about 15 minutes to make. High value. Low cost.

End Result: These types of solutions require a high, one-time cost of creation, but infinitely low additional effort after. This is what you want. This creates a scalable, profitable business.

EXERCISE #20 (Offer Step 5b): Putting it all together

Let's sum this up before we configure our final high value deliverable.

Step #1: We figured out our prospective client's dream outcome.

Step #2: We listed out all the obstacles they're likely to encounter on their way (our opportunities for value).

Step #3: We listed all those obstacles as solutions.

Step #4: We figured out all the different ways we could deliver those solutions.

Step #5a: We trimmed those ways down to only the things that were the highest value and lowest cost to us.

All we have to do now is…

Step #5b: Put all the bundles together into the ultimate high value deliverable.

REWRITE THE HIGH VALUE LOW COST OPTIONS ON A NEW PAGE OR SEPARATE DOCUMENT. ASSIGN A REALISTIC VALUE TO EACH. THEN, ADD IT ALL TOGETHER.

Below you can find examples of me doing the exercise.

Format Note

I'm going to display each problem-solution set as:

Problem → Solution Wording→ Sexier Name for Bundle .

Then, underneath, you will see the actual delivery vehicle (what we're actually gonna do for them/provide)

Example Item 1: *Buying food*→ How anyone can buy food fast, easy, cheaply → Foolproof Bargain Grocery System . . . that'll save hundreds of dollars per month on your food and take less time than your current shopping routine ($1,000 value for the money it'll save you from this point on in your life)

    a. 1-on-1 Nutrition Orientation where I explain how to use…

    b. Recorded grocery tour

    c. DIY Grocery Calculator

    d. Each plan comes with its own list for each week

    e. Bargain grocery shopping training

    f. Grocery Buddy System

    g. Pre-made insta-cart grocery carts for delivery

    h. And a check-in via text weekly.

Example Item 2: *Cooking*→ Ready in 5 min Busy Parent Cooking Guide . . . how anyone can eat healthy even if they have no time ($600 value from getting 200 hours per year back — that's four weeks of work!)

a) 1-on-1 Nutrition Orientation where I explain how to use…

b) Meal Prep Instructions

c) DIY Meal Prep Calculator

d) Each plan comes with its own meal prep instructions for each week

e) Meal prep buddy system

f) Healthy snacks in under 5 min guide

g) A weekly post they make to tag me for feedback

Example Item 3: *Eating→* Personalized Lick Your Fingers Good Meal Plan . . . so good it'll be easier to follow than eating what you used to "cheat" with and cost less! ($500 value)

a) 1-on-1 Nutrition Orientation where I explain how to use…

b) Personalized Meal Plan

c) 5 min Morning shake guide

d) 5 min Budget Lunches

e) 5 min Budget Dinners

f) Family size meals

g) A daily picture of their meals

h) 1-on-1 feedback meeting to make adjustments to their plan (and upsell them)

Remaining Examples for our Grand Slam Offer…

Exercise→ Fat Burning Workouts Proven To Burn More Fat Than Doing It Alone . . . adjusted to your needs so you never go too fast, plateau, or risk injury ($699 value)

Traveling→ The Ultimate Tone Up While You Travel Eating & Workout Blueprint . . . for getting amazing workouts in with no equipment so you don't feel guilty enjoying yourself ($199 value)

How to actually stick with it→ The "Never Fall Off" Accountability System . . . the unbeatable system that works without your permission (it's even gotten people who hate coming to the gym to look forward to showing up) ($1000 value)

How To Be Social→ The 'Live It Up While Slimming Down" Eating Out System that will give you the freedom to eat out and live life without feeling like the "odd man out" ($349 value)

Total value: $4,351 (!) All for only $599.

Can you see how much more valuable this is than a gym membership?

The Grand Slam Offer does **three** core things:

1) Solves *all* the perceived problems (not just some)

2) Gives you the conviction that what you're selling is one of a kind (very important)

3) Makes it impossible to compare or confuse your business or offering with the one down the street

Whew! We finally have what we are going to deliver in all its glory.

Important Note: You wouldn't present it this way. It would likely be overwhelming. I'll explain how to present it in the next section.

Summary Points

We now have a grand slam offer that is not bound by conventional pricing. You can sell in a category of one, and compete with *no one*. Prospects will now only make a *value-based* rather than a *price-based* decision on whether they should buy from us. Hoorah!

Now that we have our core offer, the next section will be dedicated to *enhancing* it. We will employ a combination of psychological levers: bonuses, urgency, scarcity, guarantees, and naming.

FREE GIFT #5 BONUS TUTORIAL: OFFER CREATION PART 1

If you want to walk through the process with me live, go to Acquisition.com/training/offers then select "Offer Creation Part 1" to watch a short video tutorial. As always, it's absolutely free. I also have a Free Offer Creation Checklist for you that you can swipe and immediately deploy in your business. You can also scan the QR Code if you don't like typing. It's absolutely free. Enjoy.

FREE GIFT #6: BONUS TUTORIAL: OFFER CREATION PART II:

If you want to walk through the profit maximizing trimming & stacking process with me live, go to Acquisition.com/training/offers and select "Creating Offers Part 2". You'll also find some checklists I made to make this process more streamlined for you so you can reuse for each product you make. You can also scan the QR Code if you don't like typing. As always, it's absolutely free. Enjoy.

ENHANCING YOUR GRAND SLAM OFFER

There are five elements you can introduce to get more people to want to buy your thing: Scarcity, Urgency, Bonuses, Guarantees, Naming. I will show you how I:

1) Use *scarcity* to decrease supply to raise prices (and indirectly increase demand through perceived exclusiveness).

2) Use *urgency* to increase demand by decreasing the action threshold of a prospect.

3) Use *bonuses* to increase demand (and increase *perceived exclusivity*).

4) Use *guarantees* to increase demand by reversing risk.

5) Use *names* to re-stimulate demand and expand awareness of my offer to my target audience.

Let's start with scarcity.

Problem #7: People Still Aren't Buying
→ Solution #7: Add Scarcity

"Sold out."

④ SCARCITY (X LEFT / Y SPOTS)
↳ # OF UNITS/AVAILABILITY

SOLD OUT !

Creating Scarcity

When there's a fixed supply or quantity of products or services that are available for purchase it creates "scarcity" or a "fear of missing out." It increases the need to take action, and by extension, purchase your offer. This is where you publicly share that you are only giving away X amount of products or can only handle Y new clients.

Example: If a musician drops a limited edition hoodie and says he only made 100 and they will never be made again, are you more or less likely to buy it than one that is always available? More likely, naturally. The idea that you can *never* get it again makes it more desirable.

Humans are far more motivated to take action to hoard a scarce resource than they are to act on something that could *help* them. *Fear of loss* is stronger than *desire for gain*. We will wield this psychological lever to get your clients to buy in a frenzy, all at once, until you are *sold out*.

Three Types of Scarcity

1) Limited Supply of Seats/Slots: in general or over X period of time.

2) Limited Supply of Bonuses

3) Never available again.

But how do you use this properly without being phony? I'll try and give you some real world examples

Physical Products

Examples: You can have limited releases for flavors, colors, designs, sizes, etc. "This month, we are releasing 100 boxes of mint chocolate cookie flavored protein bars." Important point: to properly utilize this method you should *always* sell out. And - importantly - make sure you let everyone know when you do so they're more likely to buy faster next time.

Services

1) **Total Business Cap** - *Only accepting….X Clients.* Only accepting X clients at this level of service (on-going). This puts a cap on how many clients you service but also keeps them in it. You create a waiting list for new prospects. The moment the door opens, they jump right in and price resistance disappears. Periodically, you can increase capacity by 10-20% then cap it again. This works well for your highest tiers or service levels.

   a) **Example**: "My agency only will service twenty-five customers total. Period." Over time you can increase your prices and squeeze the lower performing accounts out and bring in new more profitable accounts, or, you can periodically 'open slots' as your capacity allows (always leaving some demand unmet).

2) **Growth Rate Cap** - *Only accepting X clients per week (on-going).* Know your capacity per week, and let prospects know how many openings are left

   a) **Example**: "We only accept 5 new clients per week and we already have the first 3 spots taken. I have 6 more calls this week, so you can take the spot or one of my next calls will and you can wait until we reopen."

3) **Cohort Cap** - *Only accepting….X clients per class or cohort.* Similar to the above, except done on whatever cadence you desire. Only accepting X amount per class or cohort over a given period is another way of thinking about it. Imagine you only start clients monthly or quarterly. This helps you get some cadences in place in your business operationally while also allowing your sales team some legitimate scarcity.

   a) **Example**: "We take on 100 clients 4 times a year. We open the doors then close them." Etc.

Honest Scarcity (The Most Ethical Scarcity)

The easiest scarcity strategy is honesty. Almost every business is limited in its capacity to deliver in some way. Just let your customers know about it, and use your honest limitations to drive sales. If you can only handle 5 new customers this month, tell people that - *and* - cap it.

Example: "We're at 80% of capacity this week. If you want in, you'll have to let me know now. " will get more people to buy from you than not letting them know.

Fast Money Scarcity Tip

- Offer a very limited supply of 1-on-1 access to you (think 5-10 people).

- Pick a communication style you don't hate: Direct message access. Email Access. Phone access. Voice memo access. Zoom access. Etc.

- Price it *very* high - one you'd be *thrilled* to do it for - think 10-100x normal prices.

- Then, tell people. Then, let them know when you sell out.

EXERCISE #21: Add Scarcity

Products: think about

- what your actual limit is on inventory
- your capacity to deliver that amount of inventory within a given window of time

Services: think about

- Your capacity to onboard new clients or customers in a given day or week
- Your total capacity to maintain clients in your business (especially valuable for solopreneurs and local businesses with real caps)

List your real scarcity below: . . . .

. . . .

Now, list it <u>everywhere</u> you advertise your offer and mention it in your sales pitch.

Summary Points

Scarcity is a function of limiting quantity - aka - *how many left you have*.

- **Physical Products:** limited releases, flavors, sizes, designs, etc. All create scarcity.

- **Services**: Total business limit, weekly capacity limit, rolling cohorts all create scarcity.

- Never say you have a certain amount, then let more people buy. If you are limited, limit it. Sell out. Or you will lose all trust.

Pick a scarcity strategy - be honest about your limitations - and let people know about them. Then, watch your sales increase.

Problem #8: People Still Aren't Buying
→ Solution #8: Add Urgency

"Deadlines. Drive. Decisions."
— **Me**

URGENCY (BY X DATE)
↳ RELATES TO TIME

5...4...3...2...1... Done!

Scarcity is a function of *quantity*. Urgency is a function of *time*.

This is where you *only* limit *when* people can sign up, rather than *how many*. Having a defined deadline or cutoff for a purchase or action to occur creates urgency. Frequently, scarcity and urgency are used together, but I will separate them out for you to illustrate the concepts.

I'm going to show you my four favorite ways of using urgency on a consistent basis, ethically:

1) Rolling Cohorts

2) Rolling Seasonal Urgency

3) Promotional or Pricing Urgency

4) Exploding Opportunity

1) Cohort-Based Rolling Urgency

You *start clients on a regular schedule*. The less frequently you allow clients to start, the more powerful it is when dates approach. But, you trade off with lower sales the further away you are. For small businesses, I prefer rolling weekly cohorts. It gives you many of the urgency benefits with few costs.

Example: If you start all new clients every Monday (even in unlimited amounts), you can say: *"If you sign up today, I can get you in with our next group that kicks off on Monday, otherwise you'll have to wait until our next kickoff date."*

Example: Another way to make this even more powerful: *"I actually had a client who signed up a few weeks ago drop out, so I have an opening for our next cohort that kicks off on Monday. If you are pretty sure you're gonna do this sooner or later, might as well get in on it now so you can start reaping the rewards sooner rather than paying the same and waiting."*

Operational benefits: Rolling cohorts have the added operational benefit of helping you create a choreographed onboarding experience for new clients. You can add resources *on one day* to give all clients a better experience *without* covering the bill every day of the week.

How to handle "mid-cohort" buyers:

1) Option 1: Offer them a speedy personalized onboarding to get them up to speed as a "bonus" for signing up today and still get them in. I don't like this but if you need to pay rent - fine.

2) Option 2: (My preference) Explain the benefits of waiting for the next cohort to start: more time to review the materials, talk to their employees (for b2b products) or family members (for b2c products), extend payments on a payment plan, or anything else you can think of.

2) Rolling Seasonal Urgency

Countdown to a real date tied to a seasonal change or holiday. This functions the same as rolling cohorts except you'll likely have them for longer durations and fewer of them. Think "monthly flavored promotions."

Example: Our New Year Promotion ends Jan 30!

Next Month: Our Valentine's Lovers Promo Ends Feb 30!

Next Month: Our Sexy By Spring Special Ends March 31!

Next Month: Our Fools in Love April Promo Ends April 30!

Plan your year out and keep rotating them. Watch sales spike at the beginning of each month when you announce the promotion and at the end when the promotion is about to expire.

Local Businesses: This is my number one strategy for local businesses. They must vary their marketing more frequently than national advertisers. Putting a new wrapper with a date on the same core service gives you urgency and novelty that will consistently outperform the "same old" campaigns.

3) Pricing or Bonus-Based Urgency

Create urgency using discounts or bonuses as the thing they could miss out on.

Example: *"Yes, let's get you started today so you can take advantage of the discount you came in for. I'm not sure how long we will be running it as we change them every 4 weeks or so, and this is one of the better ones we have run in a while."*

You rotate the discount or bonus on a regular cadence and get people to sign up for the "extra."

Tip: If you plan on raising prices - <u>let people know.</u> *"The price is going up! So get in now!"* It will give you an influx of cash from the people in the pipeline who were on the fence.

4) Exploding Opportunity

Great opportunities don't stay great forever. You educate the customer on the one-time nature of the opportunity. Namely, that it's extremely valuable today, but every moment they delay, decreases their opportunity as more people find out about it.

B2B Example: If I was explaining an arbitrage opportunity between buying products on eBay and selling them on Amazon, this market inefficiency would over time correct itself. The sooner someone acts the better it will be for them.

Employee Example: Highly competitive job environments often get job offers that are "exploding offers" everyday they wait to take the job, their pay or bonuses decrease. This forces prospects to make fast decisions rather than try and "wait it out" to see if they get a better offer.

If you have an opportunity that decreases in value over time - *let people know.*

EXERCISE #22: Add Urgency

Create an example of the first 3 types of urgency in your business. If possible for what you sell, create exploding urgency.

Cohort based Urgency: ....
....

Rolling Seasonal Urgency: ....
....

Pricing or Bonus Based Urgency: ....
....

Exploding Opportunity: ....
....

Use the one (or multiple) that best fit your business/products.

Summary Points

- Pick one of the four types of urgency.

- Figure out the deadline.

- Let people know about it.

- Then repeat.

FREE GIFT #7: BONUS TUTORIAL: HOW TO ETHICALLY USE SCARCITY & URGENCY

If you want to walk through some live (ethical) examples of scarcity & urgency with me, go to **Acquisition.com/training/offers** and select **"Scarcity & Urgency"** to watch a short video tutorial. You'll also be able to grab my **Scarcity Urgency Checklist** I use when creating offers. You can also scan the QR Code if you don't like typing. As always, it's absolutely free. Enjoy.

SCAN ME

Problem #9: People Still Aren't Buying
→ Solution #9: Add Bonuses

"It's all gravy baby"
— Play on an old English saying.

Main point: *A single offer is less valuable than the same offer broken into its component parts and stacked as bonuses* (see image). This is why every infomercial of all time continues on with "but wait….there's more!" It works.

You establish the price, then they expand upon it until the prospect feel *it's such a good deal it would be stupid to pass it up.* With each increasingly valuable bonus, that discrepancy between price and value grows until it's too big to bear. Then the rubber band that holds the prospects wallet in their pocket snaps and they buy.

Bonuses vs Discounts: Once I present my actual price, I never discount. Prices aren't negotiable. But, bonuses are. So if I have someone who is *almost* ready to buy, I add bonuses and ask for the sale again. Pull them out one at a time and ask for the sale each time. And keep adding them until they *feel stupid saying no.*

Now, you can still choose to give every client the same bonuses even if someone says "yes" on the first ask. You just present them *after* they buy. This will have them love you that much more for over delivering right off the bat.

Bonus Tactics

Use all your offer components from Solution #6 "Trim and Stack." Each of those deliverables is now being weaponized and presented at the perfect time by stacking them one at a time. Here are some best practices I've found from my time:

1) Always offer bonuses - you won't sell *less* by having them.

2) Give them a special name that has a benefit in the title.

3) Tell them:

   a) How it relates to their issue

   b) What it is

   c) How you discovered it, or what you had to do to create it

   d) How it will specifically improve their lives or make their experience

      i) Faster, easier or less effort/sacrifice (value equation)

4) Provide some proof (this can be a stat, a past client, or personal experience) to prove that this thing is valuable.

5) Paint a vivid mental image of what their life will be like *assuming* they have already used it and are experiencing the benefits.

6) Always ascribe a price tag to them and justify it.

7) Tools & checklists are better than additional trainings (as the effort & time are lower with the former, so the value is higher. The value equation still reigns supreme).

8) They should each address a specific concern/obstacle in the prospect's mind about why they can't or won't be successful (bonus should prove their belief incorrect).

9) This can also be what they would logically realize they will need next. You want to solve their next problem before they even encounter it.

10) <u>The value of the bonuses should eclipse the value of the core offer.</u> Psychological-ly as you continue to add offers, it continues to expand the price to value discrep-ancy. It also, subconsciously communicates that the core offer *must* be valuable because if these are the bonuses, the main thing has to be more valuable than the bonuses, right? (No, but you can use this psychological bias to make your offer seem wildly compelling).

11) Anything that you can invest in one time that clearly costs time or money to create, but can be given away endless time is a perfect fit for a bonus. Ex: Create checklists, tools, swipe files, scripts, and templates make great bonuses.

12) Record every client workshop, webinar, event, interview and use them as additional bonuses.

13) Bonus vs part of core offer? Short answer: Sizzle. Many times you provide so much "stuff" that valuable parts can get lost in the mix. Highlight the most valuable ones as bonuses. Ex: Someone might not feel justified paying lots of money for a checklist or infographic, but as a bonus might be perceived as more valuable.

14) You can further enhance the value of your bonuses by adding scarcity and urgency to the bonus themselves (which takes this technique and puts it on steroids).

    a) <u>Bonuses With Scarcity</u>

        <u>Version 1</u>: Only people who sign up for XZY program will have access to my Bonus #1, 2, 3 that are never for sale or available anywhere else other than through this program.

        <u>Version 2</u>: I have 3 tickets left to my $5,000 virtual event. If you buy this program you can get one of the last 3 tickets as a bonus.

    b) <u>Bonuses With Urgency</u>

        <u>Version 1</u>: If you buy today, I will add in XYZ bonus that normally costs $1,000, for free. And I'll do that because I want to reward action takers.

    c) With hope, you can see the subtle differences. The first two examples aren't constrained by time. They state that if you buy the program you will get things you normally would not be able to. The bonus with urgency is about them buying *today*, and if they do not buy today, they lose those bonuses. Minor difference, but worth noting.

15) You can also make a guarantee itself a bonus. Ex: *"I want to remove any fear you have about making the decision today. So, if you decide to move forward today, I'll also give you a 30 day money back guarantee, which I do not normally offer."*

EXERCISE #23: Add Your Own Bonuses

Take the most compelling items from your solutions list. Think five to seven. Then save them for the end when you need to push people over the edge. Feel free to add new bonuses that the bullets above got you thinking about.

Bonus #1: ....

Bonus #2: ....

Bonus #3: ....

Bonus #4: ....

Bonus #5: ....

Bonus #6: ....

Bonus #7: ....

Reminder: You'll still give every customer who buys all the bonuses. The easy to sell customers, you'll give the bonuses to after they buy. The hard to sell customers, you'll add the bonuses before they buy, then ask for the sale again. The leftover bonuses you tell them about after so they love you that much more.

Advanced Level Bonuses - Other People's Products and Services

Offer non-competitive businesses free exposure to your clients by allowing you to give free/discounted samples of *their* services and products as a part of *your* bonuses. To find them, just think about all the other things your customer would be interested in buying *before* or *after* using your product/service. Sometimes you can justify your entire price through bonuses you don't even have to deliver on!

This gives:

Free marketing for them.

Free added value to you that you can still charge for.

Win-win.

Example: If I owned a pain clinic, I might get a massage therapist to give me 1-2 free massages to incorporate into my offer. On top of that, I might get:

...a chiropractor to give me two free adjustments. (Value: $100)

...a low inflammation food company to give me discounts for their products ($50 savings)

...discounts for braces and orthotics ($150 savings)

...a local health club down the street to give me a personal training session for free and a free month of membership to their pool ($100 Value)

...discounts on pharmaceutical drugs from the local pharmacist ($100/mo in savings)

...repeat the above for multiple service providers (so perhaps I get ten chiropractors to all give me a free adjustment, now I have ten free adjustments in my bundle.

...Etc.

Now if my offer was $400, then the value of these free bonuses ALONE is worth more than the $400. And I don't even have to deliver on any of this! I could sell this on it's own and keep all the profit.

Advanced Move: You can even get them to pay you to give their stuff away for free. So not only does the customer pay you for your discounted thing, you can also ask for a flat fee per introduction <u>or</u> a percentage of sales the customer makes *after* your introduction to them. Now bonuses become revenue streams!

Advanced Example: So let's also say we negotiated the following *commissions* for making the introduction to these businesses.

...the chiro gives you $100 per person who comes into their office

...the food company gives you free food (yum!)

...orthotics company gives you $100 per person referred

...health club gives you a free membership OR $50 per person who signs up

...pharmacy gives you $100 per person

Our $400 offer now has the possibility of making us an extra $350...*pure profit*! That's the beauty of these relationships. The other businesses will pay you and you don't have to do *anything* but refer customers to them that you have already spent the money to acquire.

Exercise #24: Add Other People's Bonuses To Your Offer

List businesses that your customers might go to that you <u>don't</u> directly compete with and what they might be willing to give away for free in exchange for you making an introduction. Use the examples above for inspiration

Business #1: .... →(freebie)......................................

Business #2: .... →(freebie)......................................

Business #3: .... →(freebie)......................................

Business #4: .... →(freebie)......................................

Business #5: .... →(freebie)......................................

Business #6: .... →(freebie)......................................

Reminder: Get the retail value of each item. Add those to the total value of your offer. As a bonus, you also might get yourself some referrals back from the business.

All you have to do to start this conversation with another business owner is ask them if you can refer them customers. Almost every business says yes. Then just ask what a really sexy promo you could give your customers on their behalf might be. More on this in $100M Leads.

Summary Points

Bonuses expand the price to value discrepancy and get people to purchase who otherwise wouldn't. They increase the prospects' perception of the value of our offer. You can create your own bonuses or use other people's. And, if you do a good job negotiating, you can even get paid more money from other businesses for giving your customers more value.

FREE GIFT #8: BONUS...ON...BONUSES

There are a million and one ways to use bonuses in your offers. You can get people to act faster. You can price anchor and product anchor (little known). You can get more people to say yes than you otherwise would. If you want to do a live deep dive with me on this, go to **Acquisition.com/training/offers** and select **"Bonus Creation"** to watch a short video tutorial. I also have a **Free Bonus Checklist** I use when creating offers. Swipe it for your own business on the house! You can also scan the QR Code if you don't like typing.

Problem #10: People Still Aren't Buying
→ Solution #10: Add Guarantees

"You're gonna like the way you look...I guarantee it."
— **Men's Warehouse ad that ran forever.**

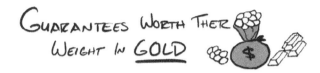

The single greatest objection to any product or service being sold is...drum roll...*risk*. Risk that it doesn't do what it's supposed to do for them. Therefore, reversing risk is an immediate way to make any offer more attractive.

"IF You Dont Achieve X in Y Time We Will...

What makes a guarantee have power is a conditional statement: If you do not get X result in Y time period, we will Z.

To give a guarantee *teeth* you have to decide what you'll do if they *don't* get the result. Without the "or what" portion of the guarantee, it loses effectiveness.

Note: This is what most marketers do. And why they don't work for most.

Bad Guarantee Example: We will get you 20 clients guaranteed.

Better Guarantee Example: You will get 20 clients in your first 30 days, or we give you your money back + your advertising dollars spent with us. This is a simple, but strong guarantee.

Guarantees can 2-4x conversions. So yes, focus on them.

I will briefly cover guarantee math, then go over the four types of guarantees.

Guarantee Math: You Make More Money Even If You Give Some Money Back

Example:

- Let's assume that by adding a money back guarantee, you close thirty percent more people.

    o 100 sales→130 sales

- But your refund percentage *doubles* from 5 percent to 10 percent.

    o 5 Refunds (5% *100)→ 13 Refunds (10% *130)

- You've still made 1.23x the money, or 23 percent more, and that all goes to the bottom line.

    o Old Way: 100 Sales - 5 Refunds = 95 Sales

    o Guarantee Way: 130 Sales - 13 Refunds = 117 Sales

    o 117/95 = 1.23x→ a 23% increase in sales!

For a guarantee to *not* be worth it, the increase in sales would have to be 100 percent offset by people who refunded. Generally, the stronger the guarantee, the higher the *net* increase in total purchases, even if the refund rate increases alongside it. Just do the math.

Warning: If you have huge costs associated with the work you do, you can structure guarantees in other ways to still sell more without losing your butt. I'll show you how below.

Four Types of Guarantees

There are <u>four</u> types of guarantees: Unconditional, Conditional, Anti, and Implied. For each guarantee I will walk though: the "if", the "what they get," my take, and scripting in the real world.

1) Unconditional "No Questions Asked" Refund Guarantees

Unconditional are the strongest guarantees. They're basically a trial where they pay first then see if they like it. This gets a LOT more people to buy, but you *will* have some people request refunds.

Guarantee: If you don't achieve X, in Y time, we will [insert offer] . . .

<u>**What the Client Gets:**</u> A) a full refund, B) a 50 percent refund, C) a refund of their ad spend and any ancillary costs incurred, D) you pay for a competitor's program instead, E) you return their money plus an additional $1,000 (or other applicable amount)

<u>**My Take:**</u> This is the strongest guarantee. But, it can be risky. You put yourself in a situation where if someone does not achieve the results, whether because of your fault or not, you're held accountable. So do the math. Not recommended for offers with high unrecoverable costs to fulfill.

<u>**Scripting:**</u> This is the best wording I've seen of an unconditional guarantee. I copied this wording from Jason Fladlien (with permission).

"I'm not asking you to decide yes or no today…I'm asking you to make a fully informed decision, that is all. The only way you can make a fully informed decision is on the inside, not the outside. So you get on the inside and see if everything we say on this webinar is true and valuable to you. Then, if it is, that's when you decide to keep it. If it's not for you, no hard feelings. You will then, after signing up at URL be able to make a fully informed decision that this isn't for you. But you can't make this decision right now for the same reason you don't buy a house without first looking at the inside of it. And know this…whether it's 29 min or 29 days from now…if you ain't happy, I ain't happy. For any reason whatsoever, if you want your money back you can get it because I only want to keep your money if you're happy. All you have to do is go to support@xyz.com and tell us "gimme my money" and you got it, and in short order - our response times to any support request average 61 min over a 24/7 time period. You can only make such a guarantee when you're confident that what you have is the real deal and I'm fairly confident that when you sign up at URL you're getting exactly what you need to BENEFIT."

[Alternate] "Satisfaction" Refund Guarantee:

<u>**What the Client Gets:**</u> If at any time they're not satisfied with the level of service they're receiving from you, they can request a refund (at any time) for the program.

<u>**My Take:**</u> This was my guarantee when I sold weight-loss programs. Besides being an irresist-

ible offer, I guaranteed satisfaction (not results). I used the strength of my guarantee to close a lot of deals. If you are good at what you do, you can use a guarantee like this to push a lot of people over the edge. The lines below made me a lot of money. I had two people take me up on it out of 4,000 sales in three and a half years.

Scripting: *"Do you think I'd still be in business if I gave a crazy guarantee like that and wasn't good at what I did? Now I'm not guaranteeing you're going to hit this goal in six weeks, after all, because I can't eat the food for you. But I am guaranteeing that you will get $500 worth of value and service from us to support you. If you don't feel like we gave you that level of service, I'll write you a check the day you tell me we suck."*

It works perfectly with a best-case/worst-case close. *"Best case you get the body of your dreams and we give you all your money towards staying with us to hit your long-term goal. Worst case you tell me I suck, I write you a check, and you get six weeks of free training. Both options are risk free. But, the only thing guaranteed <u>not</u> to help you is walking out of here today."*

2) Conditional Guarantees

Conditional guarantees include "terms and conditions" to the guarantee. Both parts are malleable. What qualifies them for a guarantee <u>and</u> what you give them as a result. Conditional guarantees you can get very creative on. In general, you want these to be "better than money back" guarantees.

Tip: If you know the key actions someone must take in order to be successful, make those part of the conditional guarantee. In a perfect world, 100% of your customers would qualify for a conditional guarantee, but will have achieved their result, and therefore will not want to take it. Also - if given the option of getting their money or getting the outcome, the vast majority of people will take the outcome (it's why they buy to begin with).

I'll cover ten different examples of conditional guarantees just to show you how creative you can get.

2a) Outsized Refund Conditional Guarantee

What the Client Gets: Double or Triple their money back, or a no-strings-attached payment of $X,XXX (or another amount that's far more than what they paid).

My Take: This is for when you sell something with high margins. And this is a guarantee to add *with* a consumption condition. That means they must do a variety of things to qualify for this guarantee. A world class affiliate marketer Jason Fladlien (who did $27M in a single day) recently used an amazing guarantee for a course he sold. He said "if you buy this course and spend $X on advertising your ecommerce store using the methods I teach, and don't make money, I will buy your store from you for $25,000 no questions asked." He claimed that an additional $3M in sales came from this crazy guarantee on a $2997 course. What's more, he only gave 10 of these $25,000 refunds out. So the refund generated $2.75M in extra sales. That's what a crazy guarantee does for you.

In general, a very strong guarantee like this will definitely drive more sales. This really serves the purpose when you need a *lot* of stuff to be done by your prospect, and, assuming those things are done, there's a low chance of the result not being achieved. Sometimes a guarantee like this can actually get clients better results on top. This guarantee will typically outperform a traditional 30-day money back guarantee in terms of net conversions (sales minus refunds).

2b) Conditional Service Guarantee

What the Client Gets: You keep working for them free of charge until X is achieved.

My Take: This is one of my personal favorites. It guarantees they will achieve their goal, but it eliminates the element of time. You are never at risk of losing the money they paid you. You risk the cost of on-going fulfillment. The guarantee is around the outcome. To add further flavor to it, you can make this guarantee conditional on them doing key actions linked with success: setting up a web page, attending calls, showing up to workouts, weighing in, reporting data, etc.

2c) Modified Service Guarantee

What the Client Gets: You give them another Y-long period of service or access to your product/services free of charge. Generally, Y should give them at least twice the duration.

My Take: This is like the service guarantee, but it ties a specific duration to your extended work/involvement. So instead of being on the hook "forever," you're only on the hook for an additional Y period of time. I've seen it work magically and keep the business on the hook for a more finite period of time which may be an easier place for you to start before doing the "all out" Service Guarantee above. This works better for businesses with significant costs of ongoing delivery.

2d) Credit-based Guarantee

What the Client Gets: You give them back what they paid but in a credit toward any service you offer.

My Take: This is best used during an upsell process to seal the deal on a service they are unsure they will like. They already like what they have, you are trying to sell them *more* of that. Worst case, they can apply it to the thing they already like. So it maintains goodwill with the customer.

2e) Personal Service Guarantee

What the Client Gets: You work with them one-on-one, free of charge, until they reach X objective or result.

My Take: This is absolutely one of the strongest guarantees. It's like a service guarantee on crack. You will *definitely* want to add conditions.

Example Conditions: they must respond back in twenty-four hours, they must use the products you tell them to, they must XYZ. Only if they do that, will you keep working with them one-on-one.

This is especially powerful as you scale and become more edified as a business owner. Can you imagine one of my salespeople saying, "Alex will personally work with you until your offer converts"? Right. It would work. It would also be a nightmare. So I would probably put contingencies like, "Provided you've already spent $10,000 on your existing offer using our structure, the offer you ran was for lead generation, and it was a free offer. These are things that would make it unlikely they would not succeed. If for some reason they *hadn't* with those stipulations in place, I could probably fix their problem in a few minutes just looking at it - which lowers my risk.

2f) Hotel + Airfare Perks Guarantee

What the Client Gets: If you don't receive value, we will reimburse your product *and your* hotel + airfare.

My Take: This is technically a "refund of ancillary costs" from our first example. I just love it a lot for workshops and in-person experiences. Normally the event would cost more than the hotel and airfare, so it's like adding an extra $1000 to a guarantee but way more tangible. It's original enough that people like it.

2g) Wage-Payment Guarantee

What the Client Gets: You offer to pay their hourly rate, whatever that may be, if they don't find your call/session with them valuable.

My Take: This is also an ancillary cost guarantee. If someone ever asks for the wage payment, just ask them for their tax return and divide it by 1,960 (number of working hours at 40 hrs/wk for a year). But no one asking for a refund will actually do that, so you will never actually have to give one of these out. Like ever.

2h) Release of Service Guarantee

What the Client Gets: You let them out of their contract free of charge.

My Take: This voids a commitment or cancellation fee. If you have a business that has enforceable commitments, contracts or clauses, this can be a powerful guarantee. Better yet, if you are in a business that does not enforce your contracts, then you have nothing to lose by adding the guarantee.

2i) Delayed Second Payment Guarantee

What the Client Gets: You won't bill them again until *after* they make or get their first outcome. Ex: Lose your first five pounds . . . make your first sale . . . get your website live, etc.

My Take: I like this a lot, especially if you have a very systematized process for getting the first result. It gets the prospect moving. It also focuses your team on activating your client. This is a great one when you know what metric or action drives activation (predicting indicator of long term retention) of a client. I've successfully used this guarantee loads of times.

2j) First Outcome Guarantee

What the Client Gets: You continue to pay their ancillary costs (ad spend, hotel, etc) until they reach their first outcome. Example: If you don't make your first sale in 14 days, we will pay for your ad spend until you do.

My Take: Just like the delayed second payment, just centered around a different cost. I personally like this setup a lot. It keeps everyone focused on getting that first dollar over the bridge. Once that one comes across, the second comes soon after.

2k) Prepayment Guarantee

What the Client Gets: You don't need to guarantee everything you sell. Instead, you can choose to guarantee a specific payment plan or option you want someone to take. In this way, a guarantee incentivizes a desired action or commitment.

My Take: This is super effective if you have a product or service many people doubt they'll complete or succeed with. Offering a guarantee as a function of prepayment, gets them even more committed. This way, you both win.

Scripting: Imagine someone just agreed to sign up. You then say *"Would you rather pay less money today or get all your money back?"* They ask for clarification. You reply, *"It's $4000. You can either do that in four payments of $1000, or you can prepay the $4000 and we'll guarantee XYZ. People who prepare are more committed and follow through so we like to encourage people to do that with this guarantee."* So now, people have an even bigger reason to prepay the service.

3) Anti-Guarantees

Anti-guarantees are when you explicitly state "all sales are final." You want to own this position. Come up with a creative "reason why" the sales are final. Show a massive exposure or vulnerability on your part that a consumer could immediately understand and think "Yes, that makes sense." These types of guarantees are especially important with items that are consumable or diminish in value once given.

What the Client Gets: Access to super exclusive very valuable service/product. Likely, this is a very powerful thing that once seen cannot be unseen, or once used cannot be taken away. Example: a line of code to improve your checkout experience on a website. Once someone received this code, they could try and use it without paying you. Or a series of opening messages for picking up girls, or opening sentences for messaging cold prospects. Things that are very valuable but incredibly easy to steal after they've been seen/understood.

My Take: It *implies* that the client is going to use it and see an immense benefit thereby exposing the business to vulnerability. It acts as a damaging admission. We have an "all sales are final" policy, *but* that is because our product is so exclusive and so powerful that once used it cannot be unused." Since it is so standard to have some sort of guarantee, not having one is attention-worthy.

So instead of being wishy-washy, lean into the fact this thing works so well, and is so easy to copy, you *must* make all sales final. They'll believe you even more if you take this position.

Scripting: *"We are going to show you our proprietary process that we are using right now to generate leads in our business. Our funnels, ads, and metrics. We're going to be exposing the inner workings of our business, as a result, all sales are final."* Note: strong reason why is needed here. Just make one up that sounds compelling. The more you can show *real* exposure, the more effective this will be.

Anti-guarantees can also work well with high ticket products and services that require a lot of work or customization. *"If you're the type of customer who needs a guarantee before taking a jump, then you are not the type of person we want to work with. We want motivated self-starters who can follow instructions and are not looking for a way out before they even begin. If you are not serious, don't buy it. But if you are, boy are you going to make a killing."*

4) Implied Guarantees

Implied guarantees are performance-based offers. Revshare, profitshare, triggers, ratchets, monetary bonuses, etc are all examples. The concept is the same: *if I don't perform, I don't get paid.* Unique to this particular structure, it also confers the upside of *"If I do a great job, I will be well compensated."* These only work in situations where you have transparency for measuring the outcome and trust (or control) that you will get compensated when you do perform.

The drawbacks are tracking and collection. So if you can find a way around that... you've hit a gold mine. Here are a few examples:

Performance: A) ...Only pay me $XXX per sale/ $XXX per show B) $XX per Lb Lost

Revshare: A) 10% of top line revenue B) 20% profit share C) 25% of revenue growth from baseline

Profit-Share: A) X% of profit B) X% of Gross Profit

Ratchets: 10% if over X, 20% if over Y, 30% if over Z

Bonuses/Triggers: I get X when Y occurs.

What The Client Gets: If you do not perform, they do not have to pay. If you perform, your compensation has been determined based on an agreement decided upon *before* you begin working.

My Take: If you're good, this is one of, if not THE most desirable setup. Perfect alignment between client and service provider fosters collaboration and a long-term relationship. I'm a big fan. This was the offer the agencies who use our software ALAN marketed. They switched from a retainer model to a performance model and wrapped that into the Grand Slam Offer I walked through earlier. I've seen countless agencies go from $20k/mo to $200k+/mo in a matter of a few months.

Minimum OR Revshare Example: You pair a revshare or performance offer with a minimum. It would be like saying *"we get the greater of $1000 or 10% of revenue generated."* So if the client doesn't generate money because of whatever reason this at least covers your costs of services etc.

Or saying *"we get $1000/mo for the first 3 months, then after that, it switches to 100% performance."* This would be ideal for a setup that takes a lot of time to get going.

These types of offers work well when you have quantifiable outcomes.

EXERCISE #25: Create Your Guarantee

Following the guarantee formula to create a few guarantees of your own…

1) **Unconditional:** If you are unhappy in any way, we will: . . . .

2) **Conditional 1:** If . . . . (outcome) doesn't happen by . . . . (time), and you . . . . (conditions), we will . . . .

3) **Conditional 2:** If . . . . (outcome) doesn't happen by . . . . (time), and you . . . . (conditions), we will . . . .

4) **Performance/Implied guarantee:** for every . . . . , we get . . . .

**The Anti-guarantee I removed from the exercises because it is self-explanatory.

Stacking Guarantees (Advanced)

Like bonuses, you can actually *stack* multiple guarantees together to obliterate perceived risk.

Example: You give an unconditional 30 day no questions asked guarantee then on top of that give a conditional triple your money back 90 day guarantee.

You can also stack two conditional guarantees around different (or sequential) outcomes.

Example: *"You'll make $10,000 by 60 days, $30,000 by 90 days as long as you do things 1, 2, and 3."* This future paces the prospect into an outcome they now believe is far more likely (since you will be deliberately spelling it out in a conditional guarantee with a timeline for achievement). Doing this shows the prospect you are serious about getting them results and convinced that they will achieve what they want. This shifts the burden of risk back from them onto us...a very powerful strategy.

Name Your Guarantee Something Cool

Instead of using "satisfaction" or some other "vanilla" word, describe it more strongly.

- **Generic Example** (Bad): 30 Day Money Back Satisfaction Guarantee.

- **Creative Imagery Example #1** (Good): In 30 days, if you wouldn't jump into shark infested waters to get our product back, we will return every dollar you paid.

- **Creative Imagery Example #2** (Great): You'll get our famous "Club a Baby Seal Guarantee." After 30 days of using our services, if you wouldn't club a baby seal to stay on as a customer, you don't have to pay a penny.

Summary: Create Your Own Winning Guarantee(s)

- Reversing risk is the number one way to increase the conversion of an offer.

- Experienced marketers spend as much time crafting their guarantees as the deliverables themselves. It's that important.

- Identify a client's biggest fears, pain, and perceived obstacles. *"What do they not want to have happen if they pay you? What are they most afraid of?"* Reverse their fears into a guarantee. Think of the time, emotion, and outside costs associated with any program or service.

- The more specific and creative the guarantee is, the better.

- Avoid unconditional guarantees if what you sell costs a lot to deliver unless you really know what you're doing.

- *Always* explain your guarantee, even if you don't have one. Say it boldly and explain the reason why.

- Name your guarantee something cool

- Stack guarantees together for even more dramatic results.

FREE GIFT # 9 BONUS: CREATE A WINNING GUARANTEE WITH ME

Guarantees can make or break businesses. They are like dynamite, they can be incredibly powerful if in the hands of an expert. Go to **Acquisition.com/training/offers** and select **"Creating Guarantees"** to watch a short video tutorial so you can start using this in your business to make more sales ASAP. I also made a **Free Guarantee Checklist** for you to use when thinking through all the variables. You can also scan the QR Code if you don't like typing. As always, it's absolutely free. Enjoy.

Problem #11: The Wrong People Are Buying
→ Solution #11: Change The Name

Implicit-egotism effect: we are generally drawn to the things and people that most resemble us.

M-A-G-I-C HEADLINE FORMULA

A Grand Slam Offer will not make you money if no one finds out about it. The goal must be that upon hearing about your offer, your ideal prospects are interested enough to take action. Naming an offer correctly determines how well your advertising converts, how big of a response you get from outbound emails/cold calls/texts, and how many inbound responses you get from organic comments.

It matters.

That being said, I will show you how to generate unlimited names or "wrapping paper" for your offer. That way it never fatigues, no matter how small your market may be. This is the key to evergreen lead generation.

Note, we aren't actually changing the core components of the offer. We're simply rotating what we name it to keep it "fresh" in the eyes of the marketplace.

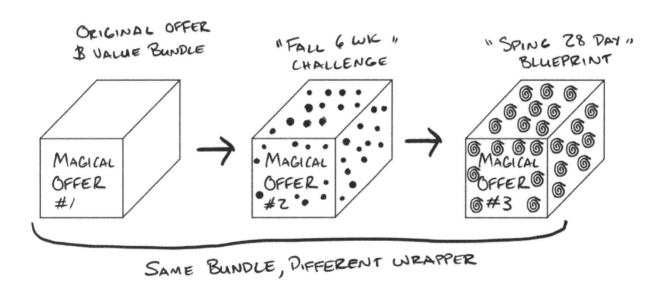

M-A-G-I-C Headline Formula

This is the simplest formula I've found to make this work in the real world.

M-A-G-I-C HEADLINE FORMULA

MAGNET	**M**AKE A MAGNETIC REASON
AVATAR	**A**NNOUNCE THE AVATAR
GOAL →	**G**IVE THEM A GOAL
INTERVAL	**I**NDICATE A TIME INTERVAL
CONTAINER	**C**OMPLETE WITH A CONTAINER WORD

Not all these components are mandatory. I typically use three to five of them in naming a program or service. If you can fit them all in, great, but it's likely the name will become too long. The shorter and punchier the better. So it's a balance between brevity and specificity. The only way to really know what works is to write the names out and test them.

Let's run through the components now.

M-Magnetic "Reason Why"

We start the name with a word or phrase that tells people the "reason why" we are running our promotion.

I like to tell people to think like a fraternity party planner. When I was in college, we had a party once because a guy got his wisdom teeth removed. The "reason why" can literally be anything so long as you believe it. This should answer one or both of the following questions: *Why are they making this great offer?* or *Why should I respond to this offer?/What's in it for me?*

Examples: Free, 88% off, Giveaway; 88% off, Spring, Summer, Back To School; Grand Opening; New Management; New Building; Anniversary; Halloween; New Year.

A-Avatar

You call out your ideal avatar: who you are looking for and who you are not looking for as a client. You want to be as specific as possible, but no more. When in a local area, the more local you can make your headline, the more it will convert. So don't do a city. Try sub markets and hyper local neighborhoods.

Hyper-Specific Examples: Not Baltimore but Towson, MD. Not Chicago, but Hinsdale, Etc.

Other Examples: Bee Cave Dentists, Rolling Hills Moms, Brick & Mortar Businesses, Salon Owners, Retired Athletes, Brooklyn Busy Executives

G-Goal

Your prospect's dream outcome. It can be a single word or a phrase. It can be an event, a feeling, an experience, or an outcome, anything that would excite them. The more specific and tangible, the better.

Examples: Pain Free, Celebrity Smile, 1st Place, Never Out Of Breath, Perfect Product, Grand Slam Offer, Little Black Dress, Double Your Profit, First Client, High Ticket, 7 Figure, 100k, Etc.

I-Indicate a Time Interval

Tell people how long it will take to get the result you promise. Consider changing time intervals (Ex: switch weeks to days). Sometimes 42 days converts better than 6 weeks. You just need to test it.

Examples: AA Minutes, BB Hours, CC Days, DD Weeks, Z Months. "4 Hour" "21 Day" "6 Week" "3 Month"

Note: Some platforms do not allow this. So obey their rules.

C- Complete With A Container Word

The container word denotes that this offer is a bundle of lots of things put together. It's a system. It's something that can't be held up to a commoditized alternative.

Examples: Challenge, Blueprint, Bootcamp, Intensive, Incubator, Masterclass, Program, Detox, Experience, Summit, Accelerator, Fast Track, Shortcut, Sprint, Launch, Slingshot, Catapult, Explosion, System, Getaway, Meetup, Transformation, Mastermind, Launch, Game Plan, Deep Dive, Workshop, Comeback, Rebirth, Attack, Assault, Reset, Solution, Hack, Cheatcode, Liftoff, Etc.

Rhymes and Alliteration (Advanced)

Good rhymes stick in people's minds. Rhyme your program name to win the game. Google "rhyming dictionary" for an easy shortcut. Don't try and force it. It's not a requirement, it's just a "nice-to-have."

Rhyming Examples: Six-Pack Fast Track, 5-Day Book Print Sprint, Marriage Thrive Deep Dive, 12-Week 2-Putt Shortcut, 12-Month No-Debt Reset, Celebrity Butt Shortcut, Get Some Ass Masterclass (just thought it was funny), etc. You get the idea.

An alternative approach to rhyming is to use alliteration when naming your program. Alliteration is when you make all (or most) of the words start with the same letter or sound. This is easier for most people than rhyming. Again, you do not need to rhyme or alliterate. Don't force it.

Alliteration Examples: Make Money Masterclass, Change Your Life Challenge, Big Booty Bootcamp, Debt Detox, Real Estate Reset, Life Coach Liftoff, Etc.

Reminder: Changing the wrapper simply means changing the exterior perception of what your Grand Slam Offer is. Your actual money model, pricing, and services will remain largely unchanged.

Exercise #26: Name Your Stuff

You should have plenty of assets by now that you need to name. Use the M-A-G-I-C naming formula to name the following (remember, you only need 2-3 of the elements to make a much stronger name):

1) Your Grand Slam Offer
   M . . . . A . . . . G . . . . I . . . . C . . . .
2) Bonus #1
   M . . . . A . . . . G . . . . I . . . . C . . . .
3) Bonus #2
   M . . . . A . . . . G . . . . I . . . . C . . . .
4) Bonus #3
   M . . . . A . . . . G . . . . I . . . . C . . . .
5) Bonus #4
   M . . . . A . . . . G . . . . I . . . . C . . . .
6) Bonus #5
   M . . . . A . . . . G . . . . I . . . . C . . . .
7) Bonus #6
   M . . . . A . . . . G . . . . I . . . . C . . . .
8) Bonus #7
   M . . . . A . . . . G . . . . I . . . . C . . . .
9) Guarantee #1
   M . . . . A . . . . G . . . . I . . . . C . . . .
10) Guarantee #2
   M . . . . A . . . . G . . . . I . . . . C . . . .

*Bonus points for alliteration and rhyming.

M-A-G-I-C EXAMPLES

Put all the components together and test it! Here are some examples for four different industries. In addition to your overall promotion, you can also use the M-A-G-I-C Naming Formula for each bonus in your Grand Slam Offer.

Wellness

Free Six-Week Lean-By-Halloween Challenge

88% Off 12-Week Bikini Blueprint

Free 21-Day Mommy Makeover

60-minute Make Your Friends Jealous Model Hair System

Six-Week Stress-Release Challenge

(Free!) Bend Over Pain Free in 42 Days . . . Healing Fast Track

Doctors

$2,000-Off Celebrity Smile Transformation

Lakeway Moms - $1,500 Off Your Kids Braces

Lakeway Moms - 12 Months To A Perfect Smile ($1000 off for 15 families)

Back to School Free Braces Giveaway

Grand Opening Free X-Ray & Treatment - Instant Relief

Back Sore No More! 90 Day Rapid Healing Intensive (81% off!)

Tightness? $1 Massage New Client Summer Special

Coaching

5 Clients in 5 Days Blueprint

7-Figure Agency 12 Week Intensive

14 Day Find Your Perfect Product Launch

Fill Your Gym in 30 Days (Free!)

What Happens When Offers Fatigue

As you market offers, you will need to create variations over time as the tastes of the market change over time. Here's the order in which you will change things to keep lead flow consistent.

1) Change the creative (the images and pictures in your ads)

2) Change the body copy in your ads

3) Change the headline - the "wrapper" of your offer

   a) Free 6 Week Lean Challenge to Free 6 Week Tone Challenge

   b) Holiday Hangover to New Year New You

4) Change the duration of your offer

5) Change the enhancer of your offer (your free/discount component)

6) Change the monetization structure, the series of offers you give prospects, and the price points associated with them (Book II)

This sequence allows you to create the most visual change with the least amount of operational change within the business.

Local Marketing

Local business marketing is both easier and harder than national level marketing. It's easier to get to work, because there's trust in the familiar. It's harder to keep working because offers fatigue faster. This is the double-edged sword of local. So if you are in a local market, expect to change the way your offer *looks* to the marketplace in your marketing more frequently.

Naming Summary

- Use the M.A.G.I.C. Naming Formula

- Remember you don't need to use all five, you can just use 2-3 and dramatically increase the results.

- Rhyme and alliterate if possible but don't force it.

- Use the six step sequence to vary your offer to prevent fatigue

- If local, expect to change "the wrapper" more frequently

FREE GIFT # 10 BONUS: Create The Perfect Name For Your Product

Naming your product properly helps your avatar know the product is for them and is valuable and will solve their problems. If you want to do this live with me, go to **Acquisition.com/training/offers** and select **"Naming Products"** to watch a short video tutorial so you can start using this in your business to make more sales ASAP. I also made a **Free Naming Formula Checklist** for you to use and reuse with your team. It also works for naming promotions. You can also scan the QR Code if you don't like typing. As always, it's absolutely free. Enjoy.

Problem #12: Nothing's Happening
→ Solution #12: Make It Happen

YOUR FIRST $100,000

"The first $100,000 is a bitch, but you gotta do it. I don't care what you have to do—if it means walking everywhere and not eating anything that wasn't purchased with a coupon, find a way to get your hands on $100,000. After that, you can ease off the gas a little bit."
— **Charlie Munger, Vice Chairman Berkshire Hathaway**

1.5 Page End Story: (Feel free to skip if pressed for time)

My heart was racing. I could literally feel each beat pounding in my chest. I clenched my jaw to fend off the knot in my throat that I knew would lead to tears. I wanted to give in. Years of emotions were bottled below the surface. Years of ignoring my reality and lack of success. Years of putting off how I felt just focusing on *moving forward*. The pressure was shooting to the surface. I could *feel* it.

"We did it," I said.

Leila, my wife now, looked up at me. She was in the kitchen making dinner and stopped, spatula in hand. "What do you mean?"

"We did it. We hit $100k." I could barely get the words out because I didn't want the tears to break through the tremble in my voice.

"Like revenue?"

"No. Like in our personal bank accounts."

"Holy shit really?! That's amazing!!"

She ran over to me, disregarding the food on the stove, and wrapped her arms around my neck, spatula still in hand.

"I'm so proud of you"

She squeezed me. I slumped into her arms. It was like every knot in my body that I had been holding onto melted all at once. I could barely contain myself. But when I think back to it, the feeling I had wasn't happiness. It was relief. I'd moved from fear to security. I'd traded feeling like a failure everyday, watching my work and effort yield nothing, to realizing a dream. The constant anxiety and fear of "what are we gonna do" *finally* be replaced by something else. I finally had time to let myself feel something.

I felt like this "struggle" chapter of life was finally over.

"Look," I said. "It's for real"

I nuzzled my head out of Leila's arms. I didn't want to look her in the eyes because I knew it would put me over the edge. I pulled my phone out and put it between us. We both stared at the unmoving screen with our personal bank account balance.

$101,018

Our gazes remained unbroken as they confirmed a new, shared reality. It wasn't an illusion. It wasn't revenue. It wasn't "profit" that was still in the business account, only to be taken out later by some unforeseen emergency. It wasn't "earmarked" money that had to be used to pay off some debt. It was *ours*. For real.

"Babe," I said. "We could fuck up and not make another dollar for three straight years, and still be okay."

At the time, $33,000 per year was more than enough for us to live at our current expenses for three years *and some*.

Years of ups and downs. Years of ploughing money into my business(es) only to watch it vanish in overhead, payroll, and mistakes. Years of seminars, courses, workshops, coaching programs, masterminds . . . had F-I-N-A-L-L-Y turned into wealth. It felt like I had broken into a new plane. The relative increase in wealth was more than I ever felt.

Tens of millions of dollars in the bank later, it was, and still is, the richest I have ever felt in my life. It was the beginning of the next chapter in my life as a business person and entrepreneur.

Some people get there fast. Some people get there slowly. But everyone gets there eventually, as long as you don't give up. Keep moving forward. Keep getting up. Keep believing it can happen.

And, it will.

Book Recap:

We've covered a lot. And I think it's important for information to sink in, that it be consolidated and restated. So this is the "back of the napkin" bullet list to summarize what we've learned so far and why.

1) We covered why you must not be a commodity in this marketplace.

2) Why you should pick a normal or growing market, and why niches get you riches.

3) Why you should charge a lot of money.

4) How to charge a lot of money using the four core value drivers.

5) How to create your value offer in five steps.

6) How to stack the value, deliver it, and make it profitable.

7) How to shift the demand curve in your favor using scarcity.

8) How to use urgency to decrease the action threshold of buyers.

9) How to strategically use bonuses to increase the demand of your offer.

10) How to completely reverse buyer risk with a creative guarantee.

11) How to name it in a way that resonates with your avatar.

You now have a valuable, high margin, de-commoditized grand slam offer.

Creating a Grand Slam Offer is the first step to creating the business you want. I did my best to share everything I know in the most <u>concise</u> format possible.

Final Thoughts

Finally, I hope this book creates a small dent in improving the world because I believe no one is coming to save us. It's up to us, as entrepreneurs, to innovate our way into a better world. And that's something I'm willing to devote my life to. And I hope you are, too.

I'm grateful for your attention. You could have given it to anything, and you chose to invest it with me. I take it in high regard. So, sincerely, thank you.

Stay hungry,

Alex

PS - (see Free Goodies below)

FREE GOODIES

I have a <u>five</u> free gifts for you. They don't lead to something to buy. They're just free gifts with the hopes you use them and someday contact us to potentially invest in and help grow your business.

1) Golden Ticket

 We invest in companies over $1,000,000+ in profit to help them scale. If you would like us to invest in your business to scale, go to **Acquisition.com**. You can also find free books and courses so good they grow your business without your consent. And if you don't like typing, you can scan the QR Code to grab them.

2) Free Downloads & Trainings

To get the *free book downloads and video trainings* that come with this book, go to **Acquisition.com/training/leads**.

3) Free Bonus Chapter: Your First Avatar

If you're struggling to figure out who to sell to, I released a chapter called "Your First Avatar" between this book and the last. Think of it like a 'single' from a music album. You can get it for free at **Acquisition.com/avatar**. Just pop in your email and we'll send it over.

4) Free Audiobook Podcast

My $100M Offers Audiobook is **free (no optin required)**. You can listen to it wherever you listen to podcasts or, by going to **Acquisition.com/podcast**. It starts on **Episode 579**. If you prefer listening on Audible, it's available on Amazon as well. You'll also find my second book <u>$100M Leads Audiobook</u> starts directly afterwards. Again, free.

5) Free Long Form Videos

If you like to watch videos, we put a lot of resources into our free training, available for everyone. We intend on making it better than any paid stuff out there, and let you decide if we succeeded. You can find our videos on YouTube or wherever you watch videos by searching "Alex Hormozi".

The next book in the series is $100M Leads. You can find it wherever you buy books.

I hope you enjoy these products as much as I enjoyed making them for you.

-Alex

Made in the USA
Las Vegas, NV
03 March 2025

18976908R00070